Family
Field Trip

Family Field Trip

Explore ART, FOOD, MUSIC, and NATURE with Kids

ERIN AUSTEN ABBOTT

CHRONICLE BOOKS

SAN FRANCISCO

Library of Congress Cataloging-in-Publication Data available.

ISBN 978-1-4521-7414-3

Manufactured in China.

Design by Rachel Harrell.
Illustration by George Wylesol.

10 9 8 7 6 5 4 3 2 1

Chronicle books and gifts are available at special quantity discounts to corporations, professional associations, literacy programs, and other organizations. For details and discount information, please contact our premiums department at corporatesales@chroniclebooks.com or at 1-800-759-0190.

Chronicle Books LLC
680 Second Street
San Francisco, CA 94107
www.chroniclebooks.com

TO ALL THE TRAVELERS, EXPLORERS, AND CITIZENS OF THE WORLD,

FROM HOME AND AFAR—EVEN IF YOU CAN'T SEE IT, YOU CAN BE IT.

FOR SEAN AND TOM OTIS, MY FAVORITE TRAVEL PARTNERS.

TO MY MOM, THANK YOU FOR SHOWING ME THE WORLD.

AND TO LISA, STAY ON THE LONG, QUIET HIGHWAY, MY FRIEND.

I'LL FIND YOU AGAIN.

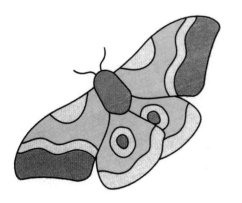

Contents

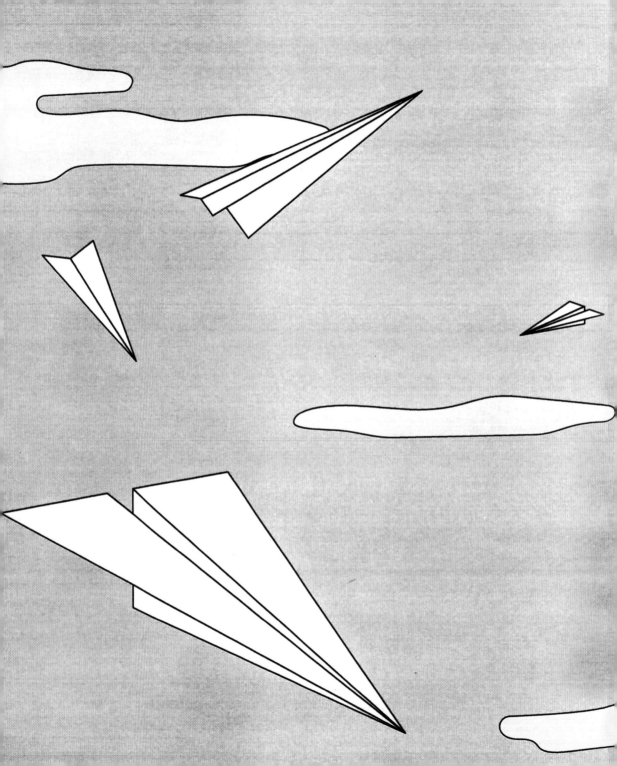

INTRODUCTION:

Welcome to Family Field Trip

MY PATH TO FIELD TRIPS

When I was a very young girl growing up in Oxford, Mississippi, my mom would often pack up our station wagon and take my brother and me out on a long road trip. We'd wind through the South, slowly making our way down to Florida. Sometimes we'd stop in New Orleans to eat beignets and slurp Vietnamese noodle bowls or ride through Atlanta, stopping for fried chicken and fresh peach pie. I would spend the hours in the car staring out the window, observing, daydreaming, and snapping mental images of all the places I wanted to come back to and visit one day. Every trip was different, as we rarely took the same route to get to our yearly destination.

When we arrived in Florida, we'd spend our days at the beach, then gather around a large table at night, enjoying peel-and-eat shrimp, laughing, and talking. Usually we were joined by family friends from abroad—people from countries I hadn't yet visited. These friends taught us foreign words and phrases, and sometimes they prepared dishes I wasn't familiar with. It was during those meals that I learned some of the Southern staples I took for granted, like sweet tea and hush puppies, were not on menus around the world. Those meals—full of new languages, tastes, and customs—made the world seem so much bigger to me.

It was those early years and my experiences with travel and culture that informed many of the decisions I made in the decades that followed. It also shaped how I went on to raise my own child. In college, I got my bachelor of science degree in Early Childhood Education from the University of South Florida in Tampa. I figured that with that degree I could always find a job anywhere I wanted to live (rather than my job determining where I had to live), and hoped that I could find a job working for a family that was looking for a homeschool teacher. I then went on to study photography in graduate school at the School of the Museum of Fine Arts at Tufts, in Boston, and

The Photographic Center Northwest in Seattle. It was those years of studying photography that really opened my eyes to what I love most about art, which is capturing the moments. I love to walk through the streets of a town I've never visited and capture the sense of the place or search out something that might only exist for a short amount of time, yet with street and documentary photography, it can live on forever. Maybe it's an old building or a found hand-painted sign, all preserved in photographic imagery.

I spent several years after graduate school teaching at a Montessori school in Seattle, and then in my mid-twenties, I got offered a job that would change my life. It wasn't in my plan, but knowing I'd never get this same opportunity again, I jumped at the chance. That life-changing call was to work for a touring band. I was offered the job of selling their merchandise for them on the road. I visited more than fifteen countries that way. When we pulled into a new venue, I would rush to set up my work so that I could spend the rest of the day exploring the city. I would try to avoid tourist haunts as much as possible, spending most of my time in areas where locals went about their daily lives. I would visit grocery and drugstores for small souvenirs, such as a box of bobby pins in India, a tube of toothpaste in Italy, or a tin of biscuits in England. I'd pop into the post office for some stamps, or the local cafe just to sit and journal and people watch for a bit. I was being paid to travel and I loved it.

After selling merchandise for six years, I transitioned to being a travel nanny for several families, including the families of band members in Mates of State and The Flaming Lips, and the family of a NASCAR driver. These jobs allowed me to go on trips that I never could have imagined. A ten-day cruise through the south of France, stopping in places like Sardinia, Corsica, and Monaco. Multiple trips to St. Bart's. Visits to a private home overlooking cliffs in Mexico. While some of the trips were luxurious and not attainable for an average family, we were often near walkable areas where I could get out with the children and explore the town. Every morning, I'd take the children through the local market as the vendors set up, then we'd pop into a foreign grocery store to learn a few food words in the local language (this was before smartphones and apps) or visit a cafe for a morning coffee, usually finding one with sidewalk seating so we could sit and watch the town wake up. Every day felt like a field trip.

Eventually, I made my way back to Mississippi, where I met my husband, Sean, and we had our son, Tom Otis. Sean was a touring musician for over a decade of his adult life. Before picking up the guitar, he spent the summers of his youth in the wilderness of Canada at his family's summer cottage and on backpacking excursions with his nature photographer dad and two brothers. Sean and I wanted to give Tom Otis the chance to explore the world as we did, and learn from our combined

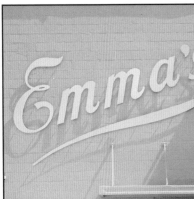

adventures and backgrounds. For our family, doing cultural activities near and far from home has been a great way to allow Tom Otis to discover new things and learn the art of travel.

From the time Tom Otis was a little boy, we've made sure that field trips are a part of his everyday life—whether it was through short lessons at home or longer trips packed with activities. When Tom Otis was younger, I ran an art and design shop called Amelia. Before I left for work each day, we'd fill our mornings with walks, art projects, and backyard bird-watching. I even started a blog called *My Mornings With Tom Otis* to document our activities. On the days the shop was closed, we'd take road trips to explore the region where we live and pack in as much exploration and adventure as possible. Our goal was to make each day feel like a field trip—fun but with learning involved.

This book is a guide to bringing field trips into your child's daily life so that you can raise a curious and confident citizen of the world. The activities and tips are not just for families that travel the country and the world. I realize that travel is not an option for everyone—it can be costly, and many parents are not able to take enough time off from work. In these pages, you'll find attainable lessons and simple tools that you can use whether you are in your own home, walking through your neighborhood, taking a day trip to the beach, or exploring a new country. Opportunities for education are all around you.

This book is organized into three main sections: In Section One, you'll find the foundations for raising a global citizen, including ways to cultivate your child's appreciation for food, music, and culture. In Section Two, you'll find ideas for incorporating art, design, and nature into your child's learning. In Section Three, you'll find practical tips for traveling with kids. And at the end of the book there are pages for taking notes and making sketches.

I've drawn on my experiences as an early childhood educator, mother, and travel nanny, and also included wisdom and tips from parents around the world, which are included as "Field Tips" throughout the book. It is my hope that this book inspires your family to explore the world together, and have endless fun along the way.

Foundational Activities for Raising a Cultured Kid

Tools and Resources for Exploring Food, Art, Culture, Language, and More

In this section, you'll find entries on:

World Schooling

Food Appreciation

Music Appreciation

Honoring Global Traditions

Map Making and Navigation

Learning Languages

You don't have to go far to find opportunities to teach your children about the beauty of different cultures of the world. This section will guide you through the building blocks and fundamentals of creating a learning environment for raising a curious and confident kid, including food, music, navigation, and more. As you move through the section, you will be encouraged to try these practices and activities from home and beyond.

World Schooling

World schooling, sometimes called road schooling, is a term that describes teaching children while traveling, often around the world. World schooling is rooted in experiential learning and uses the world as a classroom. You don't have to be traveling the globe to implement world schooling techniques—these philosophies can easily be implemented at home or on the road.

There are lots of teaching styles you can draw from if you're interested in world schooling. My son is in traditional public school, so we take into account the subjects that he's interested in at the time and build his learning around that. How you educate your kids is a personal choice, and I'm not here to tell you one way is better than the next. There are so many different approaches and curriculums to choose from; this is only what works for us and how we approach teaching outside of the traditional classroom, both at home and when we travel. We work the following styles into our everyday life because they align with our personal philosophies on education and learning.

Charlotte Mason: This method emphasizes "education is an atmosphere, a discipline, and a life." In this approach, children learn through thoughts and experiences rather than relying on textbook facts. The Charlotte Mason philosophy encourages spending time in the outdoors and emphasizes the importance of structure, order, and good habits, so that children become disciplined in their learning. We use Charlotte Mason principles for our art and nature studies, including nature collections, journaling, and forest education.

Montessori: This style of learning emphasizes independent thinking. Children are encouraged to make their own decisions and be creative thinkers. We use this approach for developing practical, real-life skills, and encouraging order, independence, and self-motivation. This comes in handy when traveling, especially when it comes to packing, taking responsibility for your own bags and personal possessions. With the constant

motion that comes with travel, it's good to be able to keep up with your own belongings, and the Montessori approach has helped Tom Otis be more responsible for his possessions.

Waldorf: This style of education takes a holistic approach to learning, encouraging both creative and analytical thinking in children. We use the Waldorf method for integrating art into our lesson plans and for language studies. For example, my son's elementary school doesn't teach a foreign language, so I began teaching him one outside of the classroom.

STEAM (formerly STEM): Short for Science, Technology, Engineering, Art, and Mathematics, STEAM uses these components as a guide to learning and critical thinking. Many schools are now adding after-school STEAM clubs, and you can find STEAM learning centers throughout the United States. We turn to the internet for STEAM activities, including lessons on physics, chemistry, computer science, and more.

Forest School: Forest School is an extension of homeschooling that has become increasingly popular in recent years. Children participating in Forest School often visit the same natural area each week for hands-on lessons, play, and exploration that encourage engagement with the natural world. Forest School students gain many important skills, including independence and confidence as they learn to guide themselves through forests and other natural environments. Spending time in the forest and grounding

themselves in nature leads to empathy for the world around them that will stay with them and carry into other aspects of their lives. How we interact with others and the kindness that we show nature extends to how we treat all the people around us.

You'll notice these educational philosophies appearing throughout the book. World schooling techniques can be used when you travel as a family or when you are learning at home. There is no right or wrong way to field trip, and I encourage you to research the techniques above and experiment with different learning styles to figure out what works best for you and your family.

WORLD SCHOOLING LESSON PLANS AT HOME

Lesson Plans and Activities to Help Build a Citizen of the World Curriculum

When I was getting my bachelor of science in Early Childhood Education, I loved creating lesson plans for my students. Building a lesson plan gave me a chance to explore all of my ideas for what I envisioned teaching my students.

In this section, I've highlighted things I like to do at home with my son that make it easy to incorporate a world citizen curriculum into our everyday lives. There are so many wonderful lessons that you can adapt to teach children about travel, culture, art, design, music, and food. The ideas I suggest here can be used as a jumping-off point for longer lessons, and you should feel free to make them your own.

HOW TO CREATE YOUR OWN LESSON PLAN AT HOME

When you are planning your lessons, I recommend building from the following general format:

1. Topic
2. Objective and goals
3. Supply list
4. Guided instruction
5. Guided activity
6. Reading list

This format will provide a solid foundation for creating a meaningful and engaging lesson plan based around a topic you're excited to share with your child. These lessons can be done after school, during weekends, or while you're traveling as a family.

SAMPLE LESSON PLANS: PRETEND PASSPORT AND SHOEBOX TRAVEL

TOPIC: **Travel the world from home**

OBJECTIVE: **To foster a broader understanding of the world through tangible items**

SUBJECTS: **Geography, Social Studies, Music, Visual Arts, Architecture, Design, Language Arts**

Suggested Reading List:

Visit the library and check out books on each place you're learning about—this is a great way to incorporate your local librarian into your lesson plan. These could be travel books, books by an author from the country, or a story based in the country.

Activity: Pretend Passport

Create a pretend passport, adding countries that you study as a family. Using poster board for the cover and printer paper for the interior, make a small book and staple the elements together along the spine. Cut and glue a photo of your child to the first page in the book. Draw two boxes per page. Each time you complete a new country curriculum, children can add a stamp or a sticker to the page they've "visited."

SUPPLIES:

- Poster board
- Printer paper
- Stapler
- Crayons or markers
- Stamp (with ink pad) or stickers
- Scissors
- Photo of child
- Glue

TRY THIS:

Revolving Learning Centers

Shoeboxes are great for storing learning materials, especially if you don't have a lot of storage space. Save several shoeboxes and wrap them in paper (I suggest using craft paper, pages from magazines, maps, or spreads from old wall calendars). Then label each box with the topic of materials you store inside, for example: travel, science, nature, supper club, art, architecture, and foreign language. Fill the boxes with little notes, toys, and tools that help guide your citizen of the world. You can refill the boxes and relabel them as you study new subjects. Store the boxes under a bed or use them as a bookend on a shelf, for easy access.

Activity: Shoebox Travel

Every time you study a new country, create a shoebox filled with items that will help your child to learn about the location. The supplies for this open-ended, ongoing lesson plan will vary depending on the country you are "visiting," but here are some examples.

SUPPLIES:

- Shoebox or other small box
- Felt
- Scissors
- Glue
- Foreign currency
- Books or printouts of local folktales
- Shelf-stable snacks from that country (from an international market or ordered online)
- Toy animals
- Folktales
- Pictures of landmarks, homes, famous artwork, musical instruments, and traditional clothing
- Map
- Flash cards with several simple words from the country
- Small country flag

SAMPLE LESSON PLAN: MODEL HOMES

TOPIC: Studying homes from around the world

OBJECTIVE: To teach children about different housing styles around the world

SUBJECTS: Geography, Social Studies, Art, Architecture, Design, Geometry

Activity:

Have children create a bird's-eye blueprint design of their own home, to the best of their ability. Then have them build a model home from another part of the world. Begin with having your child explore homes from around the world. This list is a jumping-off point, but feel free to come up with your own ideas!

HOMES TO STUDY:

- Turf houses in Iceland
- Hanoks in Korea
- Adobe homes in Mexico
- Chalets in Switzerland
- Thatched cottages in England
- Siheyuan homes in China
- Yurts in Mongolia
- Cave homes in Tunisia
- Stilt homes in Cambodia
- Rondavels in Botswana
- Spanish colonial homes in Cuba

SUPPLIES:

Let children guide the project by making their own selections for the supplies. Allow them to choose from the following:

- Modeling clay
- Ice pop sticks
- Cardboard toilet paper rolls
- Found sticks
- Cardboard
- Empty milk cartons
- School glue
- Paint and paintbrushes
- Scissors
- Crayons, markers, or colored pencils
- Paper (grid, construction, or plain copy paper)
- Ruler

Suggested Reading List:

1. *Home* by Carson Ellis

2. *Everything You Need for a Treehouse* by Carter Higgins

3. *Brick* by Joshua David Stein

4. *House Held Up by Trees* by Ted Kooser

5. *Come Over to My House* by Theo LeSieg

6. *If You Lived Here* by Giles Laroche

NINE MORE IDEAS TO INCORPORATE INTO YOUR CITIZEN OF THE WORLD CURRICULUM

1. Reach out to a school in another country to find a class to work with for a pen pal exchange.

2. Study what a school day looks like for children around the world.

3. Pick one artist, from another country, to study and have children do a full lesson on the artist.

4. Travel the world through books. Travel the path of the globe, reading books in order of each country, talking about navigation and each country on each "stop."

5. Host a mini film festival for friends, showing foreign films for kids, complete with snacks and drinks from different countries.

6. Make different ice creams from around the world (pages 48–49).

7. Study global weather patterns, different types of weather terms, and location of various events, like monsoons, tsunamis, earthquakes, and so on.

8. Have children build structures, monuments, and landmarks from around the world out of LEGOs or other materials.

9. Create a revolving learning center (page 29).

TRY THIS:

Create a Travel Center at Home

Setting up a travel center is simple. Designate a spot in your home that is easily accessible for children, like a small bookshelf or side table. Or, if you don't have much space to spare, you can make a travel center box that can be easily stored away and pulled out when needed. Here are some ideas for things to add to your travel center:

- Maps

- A globe

- Books about foreign countries

- Art books highlighting artists from around the world

- Travel guides

- Stamps and postcards from a variety of places

- Fun souvenirs from places you've traveled or places loved ones have traveled (this could include patches, pressed pennies, hotel pens, shells, snow globes, pins, and more)

- Foreign money (see the following Try This box)

- Travel journals (page 176)

- Pen pal writing supplies

TRY THIS:

Collecting Currency

Next time you're traveling abroad, collect some foreign currency to add to the collection to share with your children. You can also ask friends and relatives to bring home coins or small bills from their travels. Foreign money can be a great learning tool to incorporate into lessons about math, geography, language, and history and is a wonderful addition to a home travel center.

FIELD TIP

"We have found that children learn best when they are genuinely interested and engaged. The beauty of home-schooling is that you can be flexible with your lesson plan and take advantage of moments throughout the day when the kids seem to be most inquisitive."

—COURTNEY ADAMO is cofounder of Babyccinokids.com and the coauthor of *9 Months*, a children's book about pregnancy. She lives in Byron Bay, Australia, with her husband Michael and their five children. You can find Courtney on Instagram: @courtneyadamo.

Food Appreciation

When I was a child, I went to a summer camp that prided itself on hiring international counselors. There were staff members from two dozen different countries, and each Tuesday, we celebrated International Day by eating traditional breakfasts, lunches, and dinners from one of the foreign countries. We also signed up for games and crafts commonly found in that country, and for the evening campfire, we gathered to learn songs, dances, language, and other customs that were common to the country of the day. I loved International Days at camp so much that I use them as inspiration in my own home today—starting with food!

Exposing children to cultures from around the world isn't an overnight process. It requires planning, patience, and time, but I promise you that it will be worth it. When we teach children about cultural diversity, we help them become comfortable with traditions that might be different from the ones they're used to and we improve their understanding of what makes the world such an amazing, rich place.

EXPANDING A CHILD'S PALATE

These days almost every restaurant has a children's menu, but I very rarely order from the children's menu for Tom (and when I have, he generally hasn't liked it and ends up asking to share the food on my plate!). Children's menus usually have the most flavorless and unhealthy options—the choices are often processed, high in sodium, and full of refined sugars and fats. I encourage you to order your child's food off the regular menu, as going out to eat is a great way to share dishes with one another and try new things.

I always tell Tom Otis, "You don't have to like what's on your plate, but you have to at least try it and see if you like it." As we eat the food that he has not yet tried or is having reservations about, I start a conversation. For example, I'll ask, "What types of foods do you think children in India eat?" while we're eating Indian food. Making the connection that children in other parts of the world eat like this daily usually helps him be more open to trying new things.

Some people were shocked to hear my son ate spicy Indian dishes or sushi early on, but it's because we never treated food as something that he shouldn't like, and we didn't wait until he was older to introduce certain foods. Try to avoid assuming that your children won't like something—if you indicate that you don't think they'll enjoy it, they probably won't. My husband and I always say, "It's only weird if you make it weird." Try to lead by example. Let them observe you trying foods from other countries. Let your children see you eating lots of vegetables and making healthy choices when it comes to food.

LESSONS IN FOOD

One of the easiest ways to teach children about food is to start with what's on their plate. Understanding where ingredients come from and observing the different flavors and textures are great ways to help them develop an appreciate for food—how it's grown, where it comes from, and how it's prepared. To kick off a conversation about food with your children, here are some questions you can discuss as a family the next time you sit down to eat:

- Where did the vegetables or fruits on your plate come from?

- How long do you think it took for this food to grow?

- Did cooking the ingredients change their color?

- What flavors do you taste in this dish? Can you identify any specific spices?

- What textures are on your plate?

- Do you notice any relationships between a food's color and how it tastes?

See whether they have their own questions or observations to share. Making children aware of where their food comes from and breaking down the components in each dish will give them an appreciation for the people, land, resources, and science behind food. And hopefully these conversations will spark their interest in cooking and eating adventurously and healthfully.

COOKING WITH CHILDREN

Cooking with children is a great way to teach reading, math, and science all at once. The preschool I attended as a child had a kitchen in the classroom. We did one cooking activity a week with our teacher, and it really instilled a love of cooking in me. Learning the skills at a young age meant cooking never felt overwhelming or foreign to me. I want to instill that same love for cooking in my own son (and not just because he wants to lick the spoon when we are done!), so we spend a lot of time cooking together in our kitchen. Here are a few things to keep in mind when you're cooking with kids:

- **Don't rush.** Cooking with children is not a quick process. It takes patience. So make sure you set aside enough time to properly make it a lesson. The end result and the rewarding feeling they'll have will far outweigh the extra time you took to include them in the meal preparation.

- **Teach them safety** in the kitchen. Make them aware of the hot stove, teach them to be careful when using a knife, and show them how to point pot handles in toward the stove so they can't be knocked over.

- **Talk about what is going into each dish**, rather than just telling them what to do. Explain how the ingredients work together, and why each one is important. That way, you are allowing them to see each component of the dish and how the meal comes together from start to finish.

- **Let them taste what you are making** as you go along (as long as it's safe to do so). Tasting the food at different stages will allow them to understand the science of cooking. Of course raw meat, seafood, and eggs should not be consumed. But spices, vegetables, fruits, pasta . . . taste away!

- **Kids are messy, and that's OK!** This is a good chance to teach kids how to clean up as you go, but don't focus too much on cleanliness. The important thing is that they're learning and participating. Remind them that it's a team effort to all be in the kitchen together.

SAMPLE MENUS FOR COOKING WITH CHILDREN

Getting children used to trying foods that are less familiar will instill in them a lifelong love for exploring the flavors of other countries. I recommend beginning this process as early as possible (I started introducing these foods to Tom Otis as soon as he started eating solids when he was six months old and began cooking with him when he was two), but it is never too late to start. Here's a roundup of some of my favorite cuisines to introduce to children.

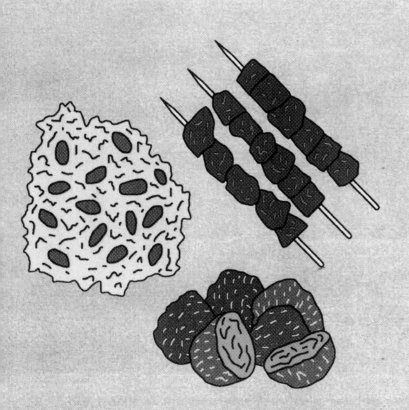

Sample Menu for Cuba:

———

Confrí or black beans and rice

Arroz con pollo or chicken with rice

Vaca Frita or crispy beef

Tostones and Maduros or plantains two ways

Cuban Paella or seafood stew

Pescado Asado or spiced grilled fish

Croquetas or savory fried cheese

Flan

Cuba is a great country to learn about during supper club. The food, the sounds, the history, the geography, the vintage cars—there's so much to discuss. When we explored Cuba during our supper club, Tom asked when we could go and visit!

Sample Menu for China:

Jiaozi or dumpling

Baozi, also called bao or pork buns

Xiaolong Bao or soup dumplings

Congyoubing or scallion pancakes

Kǎo yáng ròu chuàn or BBQ meat skewers

Dòuhuā or tofu pudding

China is an enormous country with more than twenty provinces, each with its own distinctive cuisine. When you're planning your Chinese menu, consider printing a map of China and discussing where each dish comes from.

Sample Menu for Peru:

Ceviche or seasoned fish salad

Pollo a la brasa with aji verde sauce or Peruvian roasted chicken with green sauce

Chupe de Camarones or shrimp chowder

Papas rellenas or fried, stuffed potatoes

Peruvian food is probably my favorite food to cook with children—so many delicious ingredients and flavors to work with! Potatoes are said to have originated in Peru, and there are more than three thousand varieties that grow there today. There's so much you can do with potatoes—or *papas* in Spanish—and they're an easy ingredient to use when you're cooking with children.

Sample Menu for the Middle East:

Hummus (made from scratch) or baba ganoush

Falafel

Challah or braided bread

Eggplant Baladi or roasted eggplant with tahini

Kanafeh or sweet cheese dessert

Middle Eastern food is a wonderful cuisine to study with children and provides a great opportunity to discuss a wide range of spices, ingredients, and textures. You can print out a map and identify all the different countries in the Middle East to show children how many there are!

TRY THIS:

Tips for Introducing New Foods to Kids

Let them pick new things to try. Next time you're at the market or grocery store, give your kids a chance to select something they've never tried before—it could be a new fruit or a whole new dish. They'll likely be excited to try something if they were given the chance to pick it out themselves.

Have them help out with food preparation. Pick a food or dish that your child can help you prepare—it could be as simple as a new vegetable. Talk about where it came from, and ask them what they think it will taste like. The more involved they are the more eager they'll be to taste it.

Try new things together! If a food is new to you, then it's probably new to your child as well. Tell your child that you are trying something new, too, and let them see that this experience is a first for both of you.

Subscribe to an international snack box club. Each month, a new box of snacks will arrive from a different country. Have a family snack night where you try the snacks together and discuss the different flavors and ingredients.

Present trying new foods as a fun game. Children often respond well to the joy and excitement of a new adventure.

Talk about what they like. If your child likes a new food, ask them what they like about it. It could be the flavor, the color, the texture, or the shape.

DON'T FORGET DESSERT! INTRODUCE CHILDREN TO DIFFERENT TREATS WITH NEW FLAVORS, TEXTURES, AND INGREDIENTS.

STARTING A SUPPER CLUB

My family and our friends have visited places like Vietnam, France, Spain, Peru, and more—without ever leaving our home. Through our supper club dinners we try foreign dishes, learn simple phrases, and dance to traditional music.

Supper clubs are a great way to bring world schooling into your own home. They provide a wonderful vehicle for exploring a variety of ingredients, flavors, and traditions.

Hosting a supper club can be easy and affordable if you do a little bit of prep work. Here's a step-by-step guide to starting your own supper club.

1. **Figure out where you're "going":** First, pick which country you're going to explore during the supper club meal. Use a globe or map to locate the country that you want to feature. Ask your children where they would like to travel to encourage a sense of exploration.

2. **Plan your guest list:** It might just be family or you might include other friends with children. Whomever you decide to invite, make sure they are open to exploring on this journey with you, wherever you might go.

3. **Plan your menu:** Next, decide which dishes you would like to make. I suggest picking just a few simple dishes until you and your children feel more comfortable cooking foreign dishes.

Try looking through your local library's cookbook section to find recipes, or you can search the internet for inspiration. Try making something that you have never made before. For example, if our family is hosting a Mexican supper club, we don't make tacos, because that's a dish we have frequently. Instead, we might look into making chile rellenos—a delicious dish made from eggs, peppers, and cheese—because that's something we haven't made before. Supper club is about expanding your outlook and tasting new flavors.

4. **Make a shopping list:** Once you've selected your dishes and you have the recipes, make a shopping list. If you can't find everything at your usual grocery store, look into buying your ingredients at a local international grocery store or specialty market, as they usually stock many of the less common spices and ingredients that you might need. If that isn't an option, turn to an online marketplace, such as World Market or Amazon.

5. **Gather some books:** Head to your local library and check out all the books you can find on the country that you are featuring—these could be art books, travel guides, or cookbooks. Have the books on hand so you and your guests can browse through them during the evening.

6. **Plan your playlist:** This will be the music that you play while cooking and eating. We like to find many different genres that are common in each country and we'll discuss the different instruments that are used in the music. Spotify is a great resource for already created playlists from around the world. We also check out music at our local library.

7. **Learn new words:** Introduce foreign languages at your supper club. Even learning just a few phrases, such as "Please, pass" and "Thank you," will open your children up to the bigger world around them.

8. **Make after-dinner plans:** Pick a game or movie from the country you are studying. In our family, we like to plan either a card game or a little dance party.

FIELD TIP

"Our son Jess is a great traveler. On the road, he's curious, forever willing to eat what he's never tried, drink what he's never sipped. When he turned five Jess and I began taking father-son trips. All I asked on those trips was that he sample the food and drink of that place. Once we returned home, I told him, he could go back to pepperoni pizza and burgers. He has eaten barbecued goat at an Indian restaurant in Jackson, Mississippi, and foie gras de canard at a brasserie in Paris, France. My hope is that, as Jess ages, that on-the-road curiosity will translate to everyday curiosity. I suspect that the fix is already in."

— JOHN T. EDGE is the author of *The Potlikker Papers*, director of the Southern Foodways Alliance, and the host of TV show *TrueSouth*. He lives in Oxford, Mississippi, with his wife Blair and their son. You can find John T. on Instagram: @johntedge.

FIELD TIP

"We try to introduce classic, local foods to our children as quickly as possible when we arrive in a new country. We hit the markets and load up on local goods—no 'safe' foods that they really recognize. They always love them and we binge on favorites throughout the rest of the trip. However, we also continue eating those things when we return home. It means that our culinary discoveries aren't just isolated experiences saved for vacation, but a result of how the world around us constantly changes and adds to our lives."

—LAUREN BRYAN KNIGHT lives in London with her husband and their three children. She is the founder of the blog *Aspiring Kennedy*, which offers a look into her European travels and provides opportunities for group adventures. You can find her on Instagram: @aspiringkennedy.

Supper Club Conversations

Once you've planned and prepped for your meal, it's time to think about what you might like to discuss. This is your chance to really expand on things your children are already interested in. For example, my son is really into art and science, so we tend to discuss different artists from the country we are studying, as well as different science programs or inventions that have come out of that country. It might take a bit of extra research on your part, but it will be so valuable in the long run, and your discussions will be even more interesting.

Here are a few suggestions for things you might discuss during supper club, to be tailored to whatever country you're celebrating that evening:

1. Dining etiquette, such as how slurping your noodles is customary in Japan or eating only with your right hand is customary in India

2. Games that children play in other countries

3. Weather patterns, such as monsoon season in India or winter occurring during a different time of year in Brazil

4. Practices that are different from what your family is accustomed to, such as driving on the left side of the road in England or sitting in the front seat of a cab in Australia

5. Architectural styles and types of homes

6. Notable artists and musicians

7. Famous landmarks

8. Time zones. For example, what time is it at your dinner table and what time is it in the country you are studying? Discuss why the globe has so many time zones.

TRY THIS:

Celebrate a Holiday

Consider hosting your supper club to coordinate with a holiday celebrated in the country you are studying. For example, you could study China around Chinese New Year. In my family, we love to host a Vietnamese Christmas Eve feast. In Vietnam, Christmas Eve is more celebrated than Christmas Day (many of the Christmas traditions in Vietnam are influenced by the French, who colonized Vietnam until 1954). For Christmas Eve, people adorn their doors with wreaths, decorate their tables with colorful flowers, display a big nativity crib scene (crèche), and often give presents of food rather than objects—it's common to gift oranges and yule logs (Bûche de Noël). Santa is called "Ông Già Noel" in Vietnamese, which translates to "Christmas Old Man." On Christmas Eve, children put their shoes in front of their doors, eagerly waiting to have them stuffed with goodies from Ông Già Noel, and people throw confetti in celebration of the festivities.

Sample Menu for Vietnamese
Christmas Eve Dinner:

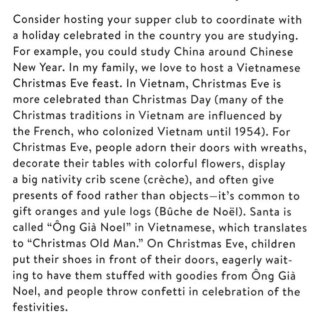

- Chicken soup

- Taro puffs

- Goose or roasted duck

- Sticky rice

- Bánh Xèo or rice crepes

- Char Siu Bao or pork buns

- Christmas pudding

- Bûche de Noël

TRY THIS:

Sample "Ice Creams" from Around the World

Ice cream–like treats are served in many forms around the world. Take a journey around the globe by trying as many of these cold treats as possible.

Mexico: *Paletas*—similar to an ice pop, paletas are made using either a water or milk base and flavored with Mexican spices like chile pepper.

Japan: *Mochi*—this treat is a mix of rice dough and ice cream.

United States: Ice cream, frozen yogurt, soft serve—this is a sweetened frozen milk fat, served in a cup or baked cone. Alaskan Natives serve a frozen treat called *akutaq*—this uses whipped animal fat instead of cream. The fat is mixed with fish oil, fresh snow, and berries.

Italy: *Gelato*—the Italian version of American ice cream, but lower in fat, gelato is made from a base of milk and sugar, and Italian law requires gelato to have at least 3.5 percent butterfat.

Thailand: *I tim pad*—also called rolled ice cream, this dish is made by pouring milk onto a frozen steel plate, mixing it with fruit or other ingredients, rolling it into curls, and serving it nicely displayed in a cup.

Malaysia: *Ais kacang*—this is made from palm seed, red beans, sweet corn, grass jelly, roasted peanuts, and agar agar, a jelly-like ingredient made from red algae.

Israel: *Halva ice cream*—this is made of sesame tahini, eggs, cream, and sugar, and is usually topped with pistachios and *silan*, or honey made from dates.

Turkey: *Dondurma*—this is made from cream, whipped cream, sugar, salep flour, and mastic tree sap, which gives it a pine-like flavor.

Philippines: *Keso*—also called cheese ice cream, this dish is comparable to cheesecake and is often served in a light bread called *pandesal.*

South Korea: *J-cone*—a cross between a churro and a waffle cone, this J-shaped cone is made from puffed corn and filled with soft serve.

Germany: *Spaghettieis*—made to look like spaghetti, these noodles of vanilla ice cream are served over whipped cream and topped with strawberry sauce, coconut shavings, grated almonds, or white chocolate.

India: *Kulfi*—this is similar to American ice cream, but with a thicker, denser consistency, like a custard.

Taiwan: *Baobing*—similar to rolled ice cream, this dessert is shaved off into thin ribbons to give it the look of tissue paper or a head of lettuce.

FIELD TIP

"I have five-year-old twins, and getting them to be interested in any food that doesn't resemble a box of mac and cheese is difficult. But I have two tricks. One, if the food is from a different culture than what they're used to, I'll point to the country on a map or globe, so that they can visualize where that kind of food comes from. Another (better!) tip is, I like to break down what's on their plate and tell them exactly what it does for their bodies. So any time there's something slightly foreign on their plate, they may ask, 'What is this good for? My bones? My muscles? My eyelashes?' That and bribery. I'm not above a good old-fashioned bribe."

—BEV WEIDNER is the founder of the blog *Bev Cooks*. She lives in Kansas City, Kansas, with her husband Aaron and their twins, Will and Natalie. You can find Bev on Instagram: @bevcooks.

Music Appreciation

Music has been a part of my life for as far back as I can remember. As a child, I would listen to Marlo Thomas and Friends' *Free to Be You and Me* on vinyl, flipping the record over and over and over. That record introduced the idea that girls can do anything boys can do and without missing a beat, boys can also do anything girls can do. It was gender equality and comfort through songs and poetry. When I'd earn a little allowance, I'd walk to the nearby drugstore and buy a few 45s. My mom would take me to music and dance events all the time. We saw B.B. King, a traveling performance by a Chinese opera troupe, a Bollywood dance with a live band, *The Nutcracker* ballet, and more. I'm so grateful that my mom exposed me to such a wide range of music, and I've continued the same tradition with my own son.

You don't have to have musical abilities to enjoy and participate in music with your kid. No matter how you are introducing music to children, whether taking them to see live music performances, tuning into the radio, or just having an impromptu dance party in your living room, music is vital to their young lives. Aside from the fun that music brings, it's a great tool to help children memorize ideas and facts and also work the brain, which makes the brain stronger. Music is also a wonderful tool to help children wind down and relax. In this section, we'll discuss easy ways you can listen to and play music with your child.

MUSIC EVERY DAY

When my son was a baby, we kept a basket of musical instruments—some bought, some homemade—in our living room that he could crawl over to and play with. My husband and I would be in his makeshift backup band, playing with him and helping him foster a sense of

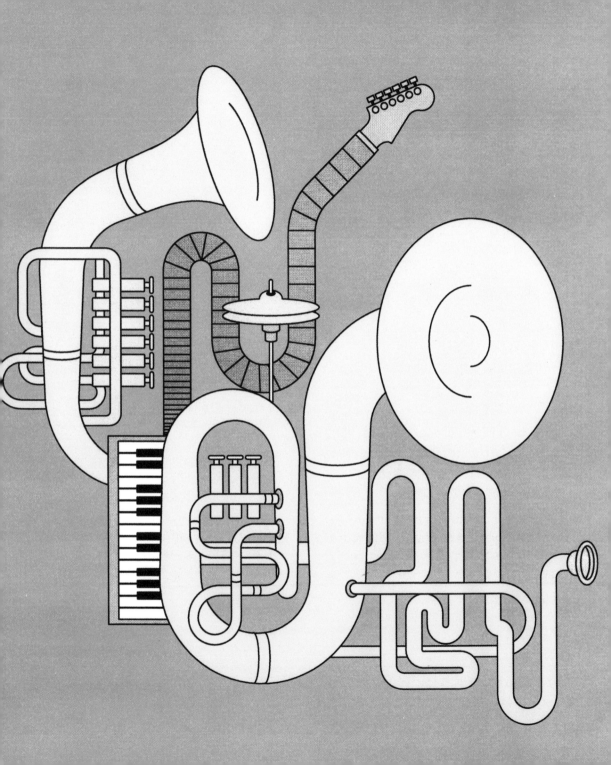

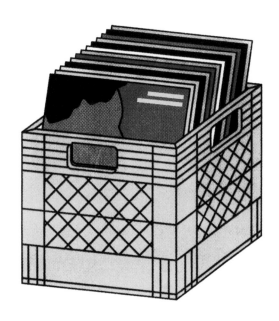

up with jazz, rock, classical, folk, pop, and other genres.

- Put on fun, upbeat music while you're cleaning the house as a family.

- When you're cooking an international meal, put on music from that country.

- Plan a family dance party, and let your child make the playlist.

- Listen to calming music during bath time and before bed.

APPRECIATING INTERNATIONAL MUSIC

As you enjoy music with your child, be sure to include songs from around the world. Listening to international music and studying the instruments that are played in different countries is a wonderful way to explore the world from home. Local libraries often have CDs cataloged by country of origin, and music streaming services provide plenty of options for listening to international music. With so many varieties of instruments and genres of music available, it can be a lot to explore. Take it slow, and find small, teachable moments as you're listening to and enjoying music together. For example, as you discuss the different instruments from around the world, I recommend going online to find video clips or songs that highlight individual instrument sounds. If you hear a sitar, for instance, use it as a chance to watch a short video on how the sitar is played. Or if you're listening to music

rhythm and melody. Eventually, he could connect which instruments made which sound, and how they played or didn't play together. This cause-and-effect approach helped him develop his ear for sounds.

There are lots of fun ways to incorporate music into your child's everyday life. Here are some ideas to get you started:

- Set up a musical basket, box, or corner in your home and fill it with small instruments. Let your child select an instrument to play.

- Listen to music in the car on the way to school or when running errands. Mix it

FIELD TIP

"One thing we do to cultivate a love for music is make 'jingles' for things we need to do around the house. It is a really neat distraction trick that works great to get your little one focused on the task at hand, while also fostering a love for music and composition. This trick works in a million ways and not only gets your children to follow your simple requests, but also helps you not lose your mind when they flip out about putting their shoes on the right feet. The best part is when you see it help their music skills and they make up their own adorable songs. This activity helps your child describe what is happening in the world around them and incorporate melody and meter to make songs of their own."

—ANNIE HART is a member of the band Au Revoir Simone. She lives in Brooklyn, New York, with her husband Doug and their two children. You can find Annie on Instagram: @anniehartforsure.

that involves a lot of drums, find a video or an audio track that demonstrates different drum sounds.

HOMEMADE INSTRUMENTS

Making instruments at home is a great way to get children excited about music. Here are some simple instruments you can make with your kids:

- **Guitar:** Use an empty tissue box and stretch rubber bands around the center of the box to create the strings.

- **Shaker:** Fill an empty plastic Easter egg with rice.

- **Small drum:** Use an old cookie tin, butter tub, soup can, or metal bowl flipped upside down.

- **Rain stick:** Use a cardboard mailing tube or paper towel tube and seal off one end. Fill it with dried beans and rice, and then seal the other end. Stick several straightened paper clips through the tube at various spots of your choice. Place tape over the paper clips so that they don't fall out or your child doesn't pull them out. Flip slowly to allow the beans and rice to trickle over the paper clips, creating a rainfall sound. Speed up the flipping of the tube to create a faster "downpour."

- **Tambourine:** Pour beans on top of a paper plate, then place another paper plate face down on top. Staple the plates together around the edges to capture the beans inside. For an added touch, you can staple or tape small jingle bells to the outside.

LIVE MUSIC

Seeing live music with your family is easy if you know where to look. Here are some resources for finding live music:

- **Colleges and universities:** If you live in the vicinity of a college or university, find out which events they have on their calendar. Get on mailing lists for their performances or sign up for email notifications.

- **Libraries:** Libraries often keep tabs on educational events. Visit your local library and talk with the librarian about what is coming up. Many libraries also have musical programs for young children.

- **Local paper:** Local papers like the *Memphis Flyer,* the *Stranger,* and *Time Out* always have a vast selection of events for all ages.

- **Local stores and venues:** You can find out about a local record store that's hosting a cool event, or a concert hall that has a special show geared toward children.

- **Town events**: Many towns and cities have outdoor concerts during the summer.

Honoring Global Traditions

Studying how children in other parts of the world celebrate special moments, like birthdays or losing baby teeth, is a great way to help your child get a sense of the bigger world. Often there are interesting dishes, songs, or traditions associated with these occasions, which make it fun and easy to get kids engaged. Learning about these traditions will help your child better understand how people all over the globe spend their holidays and days and find common ground with kids from different backgrounds.

BIRTHDAY CELEBRATIONS AROUND THE WORLD

There are so many amazing global traditions when it comes to celebrating birthdays. Many cultures serve a special dish that is only served on that day. In some cultures, only certain ages are celebrated, while in others every age is a party. Here are some of the ways children's birthdays are celebrated around the world:

- **Germany:** Children's birthday parties in Germany are called *Kinderfest* (in fact, the first birthday parties with birthday cake can be traced back to thirteenth-century Germany). It's common to wake sleeping children with cake and candles, but the candles don't get blown out right away—instead they are replaced with newly lit candles as they burn down throughout the day and then blown out after dinner.

- **Philippines:** In the Philippines, birthdays usually begin by attending Church mass followed by a lavish party. Children are given lots of gifts, food, and attention. While Filipino children generally have a birthday party every year, the first, seventh, and eighteenth birthdays are the most special.

- **Israel:** In Israel, the birthday kid often wears a crown that is adorned with flowers or leaves to signify that it's their special day. Friends and family members sing and dance around the child while they are raised up and down in a chair to the equal number of times as their new age. Afterward, they eat a cake decorated with elements related to the child's interests.

- **The Netherlands:** Birthday celebrations here are not just for the child turning a year older. The day is also about the birth, and parents and friends are congratulated on the occasion. When it comes time to sing a birthday song, rather than surrounding the child whose birthday it is, all the participants form one large circle to sing.

- **Korea:** In Korean culture, the most significant birthday celebration is called *Dol* or *Doljanchi*. When a child turns one, they are dressed in traditional Korean clothing, and presented with five to six items, each with its own meaning. Whichever item they pick is thought to predict which direction their lives will go in—for example, if they pick a paintbrush, they might become an artist, or if they pick a stethoscope they might become a doctor.

TRADITIONS TO CELEBRATE LOSING BABY TEETH

There are many different ways to celebrate losing baby teeth. Next time your child loses a tooth, use it as an opportunity to discuss how kids in other parts of the world mark this occasion. Here are some fun examples:

- **China:** When children lose a tooth from the top row, they throw it on the floor. When a tooth is lost from the bottom row, the tooth is placed on the roof of the house. Children often make a wish with the tossing of the tooth. This is a common practice in most Middle Eastern countries as well.

- **Argentina:** A little furry mouse—sometimes called Ratoncito Pérez, Raton Pérez, or Pérez Mouse—is welcomed in, much like the tooth fairy, to leave money or a small gift in exchange for the lost tooth under a child's pillow. France has a similar mouse friend called La Bonne Petite Souris.

- **El Salvador:** In El Salvador, a rabbit visits children's bedrooms to gather the lost tooth.

- **Ukraine:** When a child loses a tooth in Ukraine, it's wrapped in a cloth and placed in the darkest corner of the home until the new tooth grows in.

NEW YEAR'S CELEBRATIONS

Here are some of the ways cultures around the world ring in the new year:

- **Japan:** People celebrate with soba noodles and get together to make mochi rice cakes. Get your postcards ready, too! In Japan, people send well wishes and good luck for the year by mailing New Year's postcards to all their faraway pen pals and loved ones.

- **Scotland:** Everyone tries to be the first in this country, such as the first to cross into a friend's home. And they don't come empty handed—it's customary to give a small gift like bread, a coin, salt, coal, or a drink, each gift with its own meaning.

- **Philippines:** In the Philippines, revelers dress in polka dots to celebrate the New Year. The round shape is believed to bring prosperity.

- **Germany:** Pig-shaped candy or cookies are served at midnight. These treats are thought to bring good luck to anyone that consumes them.

- **Spain:** The 12 Grapes of Luck bless this celebration, with one grape consumed with each chime of the clock. Cut the grapes in half for small children. The grapes are thought to chase away evil spirits and bring prosperity.

TRY THIS:

Cross Over Time Zones for New Year's Eve

If letting your child stay up until midnight seems unreasonable, consider planning a celebration where you commemorate the New Year arriving in a different part of the world. That way, you can still celebrate with your little ones earlier in the day, get them to bed on schedule, and they can learn about other countries' festivities in the process.

Map Making and Navigation

My grandfather used to study maps for fun. He was a pilot for a long time and would get engrossed in studying new routes by car or flight patterns by air. He never stopped exploring the art of the map. Now, Tom and I often sit down and study maps, carrying on my grandfather's passion.

We talk about navigation, cartography, borders, time zones, and distances. Before we take a trip, I always print out a map of where we are going or order one from AAA (you can get free maps with your membership). If we are on a road trip, I often stop in each state's visitor center and get a local map for him. Those are his maps to do with what he wants. He can draw where he's been, highlight our route, or just read it and follow along during our journey. When we go anywhere that requires reading a map, whether it's to the zoo or a museum, he always wants to be the navigator. Even in the car, if I put an address into the GPS, Tom will help tell me when to turn based on the car's navigation. I always encourage him to help me by listening and watching where we are going. I've noticed this also helps

him follow his teacher's directions in school and be a better listener.

Maps aren't just useful for navigation; they can also act as vehicles for storytelling, art, and geography. When a city or country gets mentioned in conversation, find it on a map. Locating a place on the map gives children a visual of where the city or country is in relation to their home. You can discuss the road you would need to take to get there, or the oceans and mountains that you would have to cross. Or you might open up a map or an atlas and read it like a picture book, making up stories about far-off places and epic journeys.

You can create map lessons that involve geography, art, science, language, social studies, and math. Exposing children to the bigger

world when they're young fosters a sense of wonder and exploration. In this section, we'll look at ways to get kids excited about maps and navigation.

Making Maps at Home

Making maps with children is a wonderful way to help them envision the world around them and a great tool for understanding perspective. Map making promotes reading and spatial skills, too. The possibilities for what you can make are endless. Here are some ideas to jump-start your map-making adventure:

- **Map of your neighborhood or town:** Add the post office, grocery store, schools, favorite restaurants and stores, movie theater, and so on.

- **Map of a trip you've taken:** Create a map of a place you've visited as a family.

- **Map of an imagined world:** Invent a make-believe world or town.

- **Map of a location from a favorite movie:** Pick a family-favorite movie and create a map of all the places featured in the story. My family created a map of *The Goonies*, showing all the important locations the characters visit.

SUPPLIES:

- Paper (blank or graph)
- No. 4 pencil
- Colored pencils, markers, or crayons
- Glue stick
- Stickers or washi tape to denote landmarks (we like simple round, colored stickers to give it more of a clean feel)
- Scissors
- Ruler

DIRECTIONS:

This is a free-form activity. It's a time to explore different ideas and styles of map-making and embrace what works for your child.

Once your child has chosen the type of map they want to draw, talk about what the map will look like. Have them envision the cardinal directions (see page 68) that they will draw on their map. If they are making a map from home to school, for example, use this time to talk about which direction the school is from your home, and so on. Talk about legends and symbols that are found on actual maps and how to use them in their maps. Discuss why we use the keys on maps and how that relates to making their own maps.

Start out with very simple maps, and as your child gets older and more comfortable, the maps can get more intricate. Just reassure them that there is no right and wrong—at the end of the day, it's a fun art project. If you can actually use the map to get from point A to point B, well, even better.

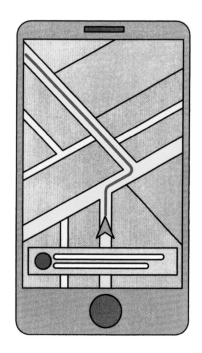

NAVIGATION SKILLS

When I was a child, my grandfather would take me on errands, and then ask me to direct us back home. He would let me lead the way, and he would purposely miss turns if I didn't direct him the correct way. Now, that might seem a bit extreme, throwing me into the deep end, but it taught me to become more observant to my surroundings. I quickly learned to pay attention to street signs and make note of landmarks where I needed to make a turn.

I now play this navigation game with my son and he has begun to point out little tips that he uses to recall places, without me prompting

him. For Tom's sixth birthday, we gave him a brass compass, a gift that he can carry with him throughout his life. Tom has been learning navigation since he was two years old, and this gift represented that we trust him to guide us anywhere. We've set him up with the tools and now he's putting all the pieces together.

Over the next few pages, I'll offer some basic methods for how to teach children navigation. And with these tools at your disposal, you and your child should be able to have fun with navigation no matter where you go.

FIELD TIP

"When Kirk and I first got married more than fifteen years ago, before we had smartphones or even a GPS, we bought one of those spiral-bound road atlases, and we'd use it to navigate on road trips. It still lives in the back pocket of the passenger seat, tattered and fat from multiple spills and years of use. Our kids love to pull it out, thumb through it, and search for our route on the map."

—EVA JORGENSEN and her husband Kirk run Sycamore Co., a creative studio based in Utah that helps brands around the world tell their stories in a beautiful, natural way. Eva is the author of *Paris by Design*. She lives with Kirk and their two children outside of Salt Lake City, Utah. You can find Eva on Instagram: @sycamore_co.

Navigating the Neighborhood

Teaching your child basic skills to maneuver through a city or town and involving them in planning your travel routes will help them feel more comfortable. Start out by teaching young children to navigate through your own neighborhood or even just your block. If you encourage them to pay attention to their surroundings and keep track of their route, as they get older they will be able to apply those skills as they navigate new environments.

Here are a few ideas to get you started:

- **Have your child count** the city blocks you cover on your walk. If you are just going around the block, they can count the number of houses that they pass. Also encourage children to count the number of steps they take and compare it with their siblings' or parents' steps. Have them record their steps, and as they grow up, see how their stride has changed. When on a walk in the woods, measure from tree to tree to see how they have grown or how things have changed in nature.

- **Get a subway map** and show them the route you're going to take to get to your destination.

- **Take note** of the street names and use them to make up a fun song or rhyme to help your child remember the route.

Cardinal Directions (or, Never Eat Slimy Worms)

Cardinal directions are the four main points of a map, noting the directions north, south, east, and west. These are also displayed by the first letters: N, S, E, and W. A quick and easy way for children to remember the order of direction is to teach them the mnemonic device Never Eat Slimy Worms. Begin using the word "north" to describe going up, "south" for down, and so on. Repeat this phrase with them when you're looking at maps and eventually they'll learn to memorize the relationship between the cardinal directions.

- **Encourage your child to be your guide.** For example, if you are walking from your home to the neighborhood park, let them try to lead the way. As you approach an intersection, ask them if you should turn right, left, or proceed straight. Point out memorable landmarks, like a corner store or a brightly painted house, so that they can orient themselves in the future.

Navigating Public Transportation

It's easy to get turned around on a subway or bus. But the good news is that if you start going in the wrong direction, there's no need to panic because there is always a train just across the platform going in the correct direction or a bus stop across the street where you can find a bus going in the correct direction.

Navigating public transportation can be hard for adults and children alike, but it doesn't have to be. There are a few easy tricks that can help you and your child get oriented quickly.

- **Take a picture** of the route that you want to travel. During your journey, show the map to your child and point out where you are on the route as you're moving.

- **Know the last stop** on your route. Most buses and trains display the name of the last stop on the route, so if you know that ahead of time it will help you figure out which vehicle to board and which direction you need to be traveling in.

- **Look at your route** ahead of time and write down all the stops that you are going to pass before you get to your own stop. Check off each stop and let your child count down the stops left before you reach your destination.

- **Give yourself plenty of time** to get to your destination. Public transportation is usually the most stressful when you're in a rush, so try to give yourself as much time as possible so that if you're a little late or get lost, it's no big deal.

Navigating Back Roads

Taking back roads is a wonderful way to explore a new place or your own hometown, and you never know what unexpected things you might discover. In our family, we love to go for long drives on Saturday afternoons with no real plan. These meandering drives sometimes lead us to find a cool trail to hike or a new spot to go swimming.

Next time you have some free time on a weekend or some extra time to take the longer route home, consider taking back roads and using a paper map to navigate. Have one of the passengers read things aloud from the map, like unusual street names, intersections to look out for, or turns to take. After the drive, look at the map together and note where you saw special landmarks or interesting spots you might want to check out again. You don't even need to have a destination. This can just as easily be applied to taking an alternate route home or an adventure into a neighborhood you've yet to explore.

TRY THIS:

Palm Maps

Using your hand as a map can be a helpful visual tool that allows children to become more aware of direction and navigation. Explain where north, south, east, and west are on their palm, and then use your finger to trace the route you're going to be taking that day.

TRY THIS:

Give Your Child a Map

Next time you're taking a road trip, before you leave, draw a map of your route. As you drive, encourage your child to follow your progress on the map and point out landmarks, intersections, and turns along the way.

Learning Languages

Learning a second language has always been really hard for me. It's something that I've had to work at all my life, starting when I took my first French lesson in the second grade. Even though it doesn't come naturally to me, I work to incorporate a second language into our everyday lives by doing everything from studying foreign language dictionaries to asking our in-home Bluetooth device to give me a Spanish word of the day. Learning a little is still learning. And though I'm not bilingual, I know enough in various languages to get around and know many tricks to pick up useful words and phrases quickly when traveling in a foreign country.

Learning alongside my son has also helped me a great deal, as learning gives us something fun to bond over together. The earlier children learn to speak a second language, the easier it will be for them to become fluent. Which language you introduce is a personal choice, but I'd suggest picking one that makes the most sense for where you live and the type of travel that you like to do.

Here are some easy tips to help you incorporate language lessons into your everyday lives:

- **Start with simple phrases:** Teach your child how to say basic words in a foreign language like "Hello," "Goodbye," "Please," and "Thank you."

- **Sing birthday songs in different languages:** Learn how to sing a birthday song from a different part of the world, like "Bon Anniversaire" in French, "Buon Compleanno" in Italian, "Gratulerer Med Dagen" in Norwegian, or "Furaha ya Kuzaliwa" in Swahili.

- **Use an app:** There are tons of great apps that help making learning a new language easy and fun. Make it a habit to practice every day, over breakfast or on the ride to school, for example, so that learning new words and phrases becomes part of your routine.

- **Listen to audio:** Listen to digital language lessons together in the car while you're driving to school or out running errands. Even thirty minutes a day will help you build a foundation for the second language.

- **Read a favorite book in a foreign language:** Pick a classic book that your child loves and knows well, and buy the same book in the language that you are studying. This will help familiarize your child with the other language through a story they know well.

- **Hire a tutor:** Look for a tutor from the local high school or university. Many teachers and foreign students offer after-school private lessons.

- **Watch videos:** Turn to YouTube for just about any language you could imagine. Watch videos while you are cooking dinner or as a wind-down activity in the evening.

- **Have a foreign language dance party:** Look for foreign versions of your favorite songs or nursery rhymes and make a playlist for a family dance party!

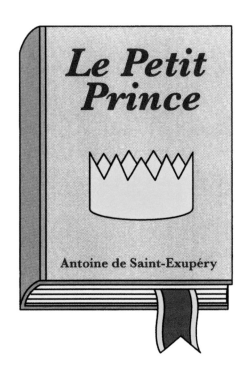

FIELD TIP

"Teaching a second language to children requires consistency and a commitment to follow through with whatever rules and strategies you've implemented. If you can do that, it is just a matter of time until your kids start to pick up the language and gain more confidence in speaking it. Don't be discouraged if one child seems to be having a harder time than another. Each personality, age, and child will figure it out in their own way."

—ABBY CLAWSON LOW is a design director, writer, and photographer. She lived in Mexico City for three years with her husband and children, where she photographed, wrote, and designed *This Is Mexico City*. She is currently living in Dallas, Texas, with her family. You can find Abby on Instagram: @abbyclawsonlow.

TRY THIS:

Greetings from Around the World

Learning about the bigger world, even from home, is one of the most important gifts that you can give a child. An important part of this is teaching children about differences, and that differences should be celebrated and not feared. A wonderfully simple way to illuminate and celebrate differences is by learning greetings from around the world. We may greet each other differently in different countries, but we all have warm, welcoming ways of saying "Hello." Below are a few greetings from around the world that you can practice with your children:

India and Nepal: *Namaste* (nuhm-uh-stay) followed by a simple prayer-like gesture with palms pressed together, called *pranamasana.*

Portugal: *Olá* (oh-lah) for hello, followed by a handshake and direct eye contact.

Australia: A simple "hello" is sufficient. But don't use Mr. or Ms.—Australians tend to be less formal about these things.

Vietnam: *Xin chào* (sin chow), along with a handshake and a slight head bow.

Mexico: *Buenos días* (bway-nos dee-ahs) for morning greetings, *buenas tardes* (bway-nas tar-days) for afternoon greetings, and *buenas noches* (bway-nas no-chays) for evening greetings. Greetings are usually followed by a handshake or a quick kiss on the cheek.

France: *Bonjour* (bohn-zhoor) for "good morning" and *bonsoir* (bohn-suahr) for "good evening." Friends and acquaintances also give three kisses on the cheeks: left, right, left.

Iceland: A friendly nod or a quick handshake, followed by *halló halló* (hah-low hah-low) or *góðan daginn* (go-thah-n die-in), which means "good day."

Tanzania: *Hujambo* (hoo-jam-boh) for hello, followed by *Habari gani?* (hah-bah-ree gah-nee), which means "How are you?" in Swahili.

男士老人
剪髮 $5
剃鬚加 $3
染髮加剪
$18

SECTION TWO:

Cultivating Wonder

Finding Wonderment in Art, Architecture, and Nature

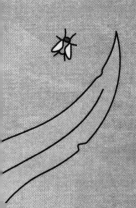

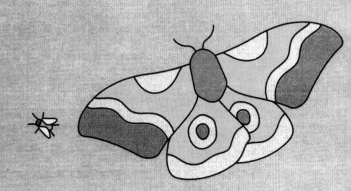

In this section, you'll find entries on:

Instilling a Sense of Wonder

Art and Design Appreciation

Architecture Appreciation

Exploring Nature

Wonder is one of the best tools you can use when you're traveling with children. Kids already carry wonder with them wherever they go, and encouraging that feeling of wonder will help you make travel with children one of the most amazing experiences you can share as a family.

Wonder is that feeling of awe when you find something remarkable or beautiful and it sparks feelings of curiosity and excitement. It could be the view from the top of a building in a city, or staring up at an impressive structure and marveling at its design. Or the feeling of seeing a big waterfall, or the experience of watching the sunset through an airplane window.

In this section, we'll discuss ways to cultivate a sense of wonder and how that can be applied to learning about art, design, and nature.

Instilling a Sense of Wonder

We live in a time where children are often so rushed, from school to activity to activity to dinner to bath to bed. But opportunities for wonder are all around us, all the time. You just have to be open to it.

There are so many everyday things that you can do with your children to instill wonder, whether while traveling or at home, to encourage them to be curious about the world. Building wonder into daily life can be as simple as slowing things down and making room in the day for your children to be still, observe the world around them, and ask questions. For example, when you are in the car, encourage your children to look up at the sky. Often on road trips, my son will tell me he just feels like looking out the window for a while. I catch him making note of the trees, the clouds in the sky, the birds overhead. I can read the wonderment on his face, and seeing it through his eyes gives me so much joy. When we travel, we love to get up early and take our time walking around and exploring a new place, not rushing from one thing to the next. Sometimes we'll even watch the sunrise as we listen to the sounds of a place greeting a new day.

TRY THIS:

Finding Wonder as an Adult

Here's a little practice to help you get into a wonder mind-set: Think back to your childhood and something you were curious about. For example, I used to spend a lot of time wondering about clouds, birds, and dreams. I would think about where dreams go when you wake up, or what it would be like to lie on a cloud or fly like a bird.

Think back to what gave you that sense of amazement. Now think about how to apply that to children when you travel. What little details can you point out to them to foster a sense of wonder? Maybe it's the way fresh snow hangs on a tree, or a flock of birds migrates across a city park, or holiday lights sparkle at an outdoor market. Do not be afraid to slow down. It's OK if you don't pack in every sightseeing excursion on a trip. Stay curious and make time for wonder.

TRY THIS:

Day of Yes

Next time you have a free day together as a family, plan a "Day of Yes." In this activity, inspired by TV producer Lindsey Weidhorn, each family member gets to pick something fun to do and everyone has to say yes, then the next person picks something and everyone says yes, and so on until everyone has a chance to pick an activity (all suggestions are within reason, of course). It could be getting an ice cream, visiting a local museum, or going to a movie. It's a great way to try new things as a family, and children will enjoy coming up with their own fun ideas (and hearing you say "Yes!").

FIELD TIP

"We are always trying to bring the elements of wonder from outside to inside. We try to find our children's strengths and develop that within them. We include them in our work, too. The more you involve your children in life outside your home, the more you let them see how you work and what it's like out there. We also provide a lot of balance, from city to country life. We appreciate boredom, slowing down, picking raspberries, looking for frogs. It gives them freedom to choose what kind of life they want for themselves and keeps them grounded."

—JESSE CHAMBERLIN MARBLE is a stylist and photographer. She lives in Los Angeles, California, with her husband Jimmy and their three children. You can find her on Instagram: @JesseChamberlinMarble.

PLACES TO LOOK FOR WONDER AND ENCOURAGE IT IN YOUR CHILD

In the woods or a park:

———

Turn over rocks to see what lives underneath.

Look for animal tracks.

Watch the sunlight come through the trees.

Look for birds' nests and talk about the birds that live there.

Look for leaves or rocks that are shaped like familiar objects, such as a heart.

On public transportation and in the car:

———

Look out the window for things your child has never seen before.

Stop at roadside attractions.

Take a route you've never taken before, just for fun.

Get your child a disposable camera and let them take pictures through the window.

In a city:

Go to the top of a tall building and look at the city beneath you. See whether your child can spot playgrounds or places they've been. Or pick a place and then see whether you can find it together when you're back on the ground.

As you pass buildings, have your child look up and spot cool design elements, such as Art Deco details or a crest above the entryway.

Look for sculptures and other public works of art.

Throw a penny into a fountain and make a wish.

At the beach:

Look for sand dollars, shells, and crabs.

Explore tide pools and observe the creatures that make their home there.

Gather sea glass or driftwood.

Build a large sandcastle and decorate it with found objects.

Sit and watch the waves.

Fly a kite.

Art and Design Appreciation

You don't have to be an artist or a designer to teach your children to appreciate art and design. Helping your children develop a love of art and design encourages them to consider the deeper meaning of things, fosters observational skills, and allows them to consider different perspectives.

Cultivating art appreciation in your children from a young age will open their minds to abstract concepts—a skill that will stay with them into adulthood—and provide opportunities to discuss history, materials, perspective, and artistic movements. I believe that we should treat design with the same appreciation as fine art. Design is woven into every part of our lives, from the shape of our chairs, to the construction of our cars, to the typography in our books, and everything in between. Teaching children to notice design choices will open their eyes to all the ways that design impacts the world around them.

To teach art appreciation it's important to be passionate about what you are teaching. While it might seem logical to begin with the classic examples from art history, I recommend starting off by teaching your children about works that you yourself love and want to know more about. Foster your own sense of wonder so that you can pass that along in your lessons. Once they have developed a solid foundation for learning about and discussing art, then you can move on to the classics.

Get creative with your art lessons—art appreciation doesn't have to mean standing in front of a painting at a museum. If you're discussing Jackson Pollock, for example, let your child go crazy with art supplies and a canvas. If you're talking about Henri Matisse, encourage your children to go into their closets and pick some fun fabrics that they can try to re-create in their own painting.

FIELD TIP

"Appreciate art! Look at it. Listen to it. Talk about it. Create it. I think our kids will appreciate art if we as parents appreciate art. I grew up in a creative family. My mother was a portrait artist and my dad a music-loving and -playing theologian. Any time we kids wanted to draw or sew or make videos—for instance, a short comedic film entitled *Attack of the Killer Basset Hound*—my parents always obliged and never discouraged us or the mess that ensued. My older brother and sister are also artistic, and I, being the youngest, had the advantage of watching and learning from all of them. I knew from a young age that art was my thing. It was just in me, the love of the arts and the desire to create."

—HANNAH CARPENTER is an artist and the creator of Little-Biscuits Notepads. She is based in Arkansas, where she lives with her husband Heath and their four children. You can find Hannah on Instagram: @hannahacarpenter.

SAMPLE LESSON PLAN: MUSEUM EXHIBIT SCAVENGER HUNT

Lesson plans don't have to be complicated or time-consuming. The point is to engage with your children, get them involved in the learning process, and have fun exploring together. Here's a simple lesson plan that can be done at a museum locally or when you're traveling. It requires a little planning and research on the front end, but once you are in the museum, it's worth it. You can adapt this plan to work at most exhibits and educational spaces, including aquariums, historical sites, planetariums, and more.

TOPIC: **Experiencing art in a fun and interactive way**

OBJECTIVE: **To engage children in the experience of talking about art, observing art, and feeling engaged in museum visits**

SUBJECTS: **Art Appreciation, Art History, Social Studies, World History**

Activity:

Spend some time on the museum website to view their visiting exhibitions and permanent collection. Then make a list of scavenger hunt items, and create a printout for each child with open-ended descriptions, such as "Find a painting that is mostly blue" or "Find a piece of art with fruit in it." Include a few finds for each room of the museum to keep them engaged throughout the whole tour. For younger children, you can include a picture key. Have a small prize at the end of the hunt for all children, as there doesn't need to be a "winner." For example, you can buy a treat from the museum gift shop or a new set of crayons. If you are visiting a museum while out of town and don't have time to print the instructions for the hunt before your trip, you can use the hotel business center to print your materials.

SUPPLIES:

- Printer
- Paper
- Writing tools
- Small prize
- Stickers

Suggested Reading List:

1. *Speeding Down the Spiral: An Artful Adventure* by Deborah Goodman Davis

2. You Can't Take a Balloon . . . series by Jacqueline Preiss Weitzman

3. *A Is for Artist: A Getty Museum Alphabet* by John Harris

4. *Going to the Getty* by Vivian Walsh

5. *Smithsonian: Timelines of Everything* by DK

6. *The Museum Book: A Guide to Strange and Wonderful Collections* by Jan Mark

VISITING MUSEUMS

Museums are a fantastic resource for building art appreciation and, thanks to the internet, you can now virtually visit just about any museum collection in the world. Many public libraries also offer free museum passes to their patrons!

When you are exploring a museum with an art collection, think ahead to how to build fun art lessons into your visit. This might mean doing some advance research on what activities the institution offers for children, or creating lesson plans that involve the works on display. If you're visiting a museum in person, ask each member of your group to pick their favorite piece in each room and share what they like about it. Be sure to pack a notebook or paper and some colored pencils so that your child can write about the experience or draw some of their favorite pieces of art.

PUBLIC ART

Public art takes many forms—murals, sculptures, mosaics, fountains—and can reveal so much about a place. These works make art more accessible, inviting, and less intimidating to the general public. I love this quote from Penny Balkin Bach's book *Public Art of Philadelphia*: "Public art is a part of our public history, part of our evolving culture and our collective memory. It reflects and reveals our society and adds meaning to our cities. As artists respond to our times, they reflect their inner vision to the outside world, and they create a chronicle of our public experience."

I remember visiting New York City for the first time as a child and seeing street art by the now-famous artist Keith Haring in the subway and on maps and garbage cans around the city. I was only ten and I still remember feeling how art was literally all around me. Seeing these urban works of art *as art* opened my mind up to the idea that the streets are an extension of the artist's canvas.

FIELD TIP

"I recommend that parents encourage art appreciation by just having it around—whether it's on your walls or in books. Kids will pick up on your enthusiasm for art. My daughter always came to museums and galleries with us. One of the ways I used to involve her in it was to play 'What's your favorite?' and have her pick between different works. When she was just three or four, we would go to the neighborhood coffee shop together every week and work on drawings. She would also hang out with me in my studio and we'd listen to music together and dance while I worked."

— MIKE PRATER is a painter living in Memphis, Tennessee, with his wife Lauren. You can find Mike on Instagram: @daddiomp.

FIELD TIP

"My family always discusses art as beneficial, for us as individuals and for society and culture at large. So when we're out where art can be found, even the art and design in nature, we try to make sure it's not lost on our children. Even if we don't particularly care for a specific piece or type of art, we still acknowledge it and talk about it."

—HANNAH CARPENTER is an artist and the creator of Little-Biscuits Notepads. She is based in Arkansas, where she lives with her husband Heath and their four children. You can find Hannah on Instagram: @hannahacarpenter.

Every time you visit a town or city you can look for works of public art. Then you can talk to your child about the social significance of the work and discuss community values, social issues, and artistic forms. Does the work represent a larger meaning of something happening in the local area or in the country? How is it helping bring local people together? Does it look like it's been there for a long time, or is it a new work? Does it look like it's part of a larger art project (some places commission local artists to put their own spin on the same sculpture, such as a fish, an elephant, or a tiger, and then place the works throughout the city)? Next time you walk by a piece of art with your child, don't miss the opportunity to have a meaningful conversation together.

The beauty of public art is that it's all around you. When you are traveling, you can often find great works of art in areas near universities and city centers. Museums sometimes list works of art in their cities so visitors can take self-guided walking tours; use museum websites and information desks and local tourist bureaus as resources. When you spot public art, have your child sit down to sketch the art in their travel journal (page 176) or trace a portion of the art. Be sure to use tools that won't damage the artwork. Then have them fill in the colors and patterns on their paper, creating their own versions of the artwork. This is a great time to talk about how artists develop specific styles, and how to be inspired by others' art without copying or stealing their ideas.

Recognizing the Beauty in Street Art

Street art and graffiti, once rejected as forms of vandalism, are now more positively embraced. Artists like Banksy, M. Chat, Shepard Fairey, Saber, Barry McGee, Taki 183, Jean-Michel Basquiat, and Lady Pink have helped people see graffiti as a meaningful, beautiful form of artwork, and galleries and museums around the world are exhibiting the work of graffiti artists.

Architecture Appreciation

For as long as I can remember, I wanted to be an architect when I grew up. I would spend hours and hours creating floor plans, drawing make-believe homes, and imagining how the home would sit on the fictional property. But I had a teacher that told me that girls aren't *good* at math, and you had to be *great* in math to be an architect. That one teacher changed the course of my life, and I ended up going down a different path. I'm very happy with how my life and career have worked out, but that experience has impacted how I talk to children about their interests and dreams.

Architecture is a form of art, one that should never be overlooked when you're out and about in the world with your child. It's a gift that is literally built all around us. When you are traveling with your child, whether on a road trip through small towns or walking through big cities, you can study and spot architecture everywhere. Encourage your child to notice the details, talk about the materials used, and discuss why homes and buildings are constructed in certain ways because of the land, the climate, and the surroundings.

HOME DESIGN

From self-guided driving and walking tours to expert tours, there are lots of ways to explore home design in a city or town. If you're considering a guided tour, it's important to check in with your child and see whether they are up for it. Let them know how long it will be, and what to expect along the way. You don't want to be disappointed or disappoint others on the tour if your child isn't ready for the experience.

Self-guided tours are a great way to create a flexible itinerary, one that allows you to spend as much or as little time as you want observing each home on your tour. As you walk or drive, point out different structures to your child and discuss the styles of homes and details in the design. Here are some ideas for things you can discuss:

- How does the home sit on the property? Does it make use of natural light or is it nestled in the trees?

- Discuss the style of architecture you are looking at and how it fits into the location.

- What kind of materials were used to build the home?

- Are there any special details that you can spot, like stained glass windows, carved banisters, or other decorative elements?

- How many bedrooms do you think it has?

- Does it look like the other homes on the street? What makes it different or similar?

- How old do you think the house is? What clues are you using to figure out how old it is?

VISITING FAMOUS LANDMARKS

Visiting famous landmarks is a wonderful way to discuss history, art, design, and culture with your child. And while you might think famous monuments and landmarks like the Statue of Liberty, the Great Wall of China, or the Roman Colosseum are touristy spots to avoid when you travel, they are so much more than that once you are there in person. Braving a long line or a crowd is usually worth it for the ultimate experience of seeing these places up

close, and when you visit these historically significant areas, you are opening up your child's world immensely. Even if you can't make it there physically, there are wonderful resources to explore famous sites online or through books.

Whether you're visiting in person or through other resources, here are some questions you can pose that will help your child make the most of your "visit":

- What was the purpose of this building?

- What materials are the structure made from?

- How old do you think it is?

- How long do you think it took to build it?

- Why do you think it was built in this particular spot?

- Why do you think this structure has lasted for so long?

PLAYING WITH ARCHITECTURE

Architecture might seem boring or inaccessible to children, but there are tons of ways to make it fun and engaging. In fact, most kids are probably already thinking about architecture and structural design when they're playing. Here are some easy activities to get kids excited about architecture:

- Build a fort, using cardboard boxes, cushions, pillows, or sheets. Talk about how you need to support the walls and ceiling to get children thinking about the basic building blocks of a structure.

- Keep wooden blocks, LEGOs, and magnetic blocks on hand and let your child build in an open-ended way. Let them guide the building they want to create.

- Have them draw an imagined structure, using paper, a pencil, and a ruler. This can be a home, a building, a castle, a tree house, or even the imagined space of their favorite book or superhero character.

- Build a birdhouse or a dollhouse together. Have them talk about and sketch their plans for the structure before they start building.

- Build a gingerbread house at holiday time. If you're working with a kit, read through the instructions together. If you're making a homemade version, talk through the materials and pieces you'll need and have them take the lead on making the list.

TRY THIS:

Architects to Study

It's fun and easy to study architecture from home. You can look at famous buildings together online (many have 3-D tours available) or print them out for discussion. These visionary architects will provide plenty of inspiration for any architecture lesson:

- Luis Barragán

- Charles and Ray Eames

- George Nakashima

- Frank Lloyd Wright

- Florence Knoll

- Zaha Hadid

TRY THIS:

Build It Together

If you can't visit an architectural site in person, you and your child can explore the structure from home by building it yourselves. My son and I love to build with the LEGO Architecture series—LEGO sets that allow you to build famous structures from all over the world. We have created a world of wonder from these tiny works.

FIELD TIP

"My favorite resource has been the website
Teacherspayteachers.com. Before we traveled to Japan, we
downloaded slideshows, coloring pages, and coloring pack-
ets to help give our children a brief overview of the country
at their level. As we traveled, we always had contests to see
who could discern whether a building was a Shinto shrine
or a Buddhist temple. We also give our kids little journals
to scrapbook and write in as we go. Train rides and flights
are the perfect time to paste in a flyer from the museum
and write about it. I'll never forget my daughter sketching
out the Colosseum while we were actually sitting in the
Colosseum."

—ELLE ROWLEY is the founder of Solly Baby Wrap. She, her husband Jared, and their four children live in Southern California. You can find Elle on Instagram: @Ellerowley.

Architecture Bingo

When you are out and about in your neighborhood or visiting a new place, encourage your child to be on the lookout for different types of architectural details. Make it fun with a game of bingo.

To create a bingo board, draw nine squares on a sheet of paper or cardboard. Leave the center spot as a free spot. Then fill in the board with things to look for on your outing, for example:

- Front porch
- Window shutters
- Wooden shingles
- Tiled roof
- Arched doorway
- Bay window
- Stained glass
- Columns

Your child might not get everything on the bingo board in your first outing, so keep the board in the car for future trips and the chance to complete the game. If your child is younger, they might not yet be familiar with the terms above so to help them, you can print pictures of what they're looking for and glue those to the bingo board. As you travel or explore your neighborhood, keep a running list of new architectural elements that you spot together so that you're incorporating new architectural terms into their learning.

Exploring Nature

When my son was really little, my husband and I made a point to take him to the woods. We treated the woods like an outdoor classroom for him, talking about the birds we saw, looking for bugs under fallen trees, and finding animal tracks in the mud. It gave him a sense of peace with the nature around him. We called visiting the woods "the trails." Now that he's older we walk for hours on the trails, all at different times of the year. Returning to the same area again and again allows us to observe how the same tree looks throughout the year, how water levels change, and how the bugs and wildlife differ season by season. We look for little pieces of nature that we can catalog in tiny jars when we return home, with the date and place where everything was found labeled on the lid. That way, we can carefully study each thing we've found and we are also left with a natural little souvenir as a remembrance of our adventure.

Although we live in a small town surrounded by nature, I also want my son to understand that there are many other ways to experience the outdoors. So we seek out nature when we travel to large cities, sometimes in the form of museums, like the Natural History Museum in New York City or the Insectarium in New Orleans. Other times we'll picnic in a city park and spend an afternoon exploring the park's fields, trees, and ponds.

Exposing children to nature is just as important as exposing them to art, culture, food, and music. Spending time in the natural world is a great way to teach children about being stewards of our planet and how their actions

can have a direct impact on the environment. And spending time in the outdoors doesn't have to involve traveling a long distance. You can learn about nature by visiting a city park, studying the plants in your backyard, or watching the stars at night.

BUILDING A NATURE CENTER AT HOME

Like the home travel center (page 32), creating a nature center in your home is a fun and easy way to bring experiential learning into your life by bringing home natural objects. There are many ways that you can organize your nature center: by season, by object (like shells, leaves, rocks), or by natural environment (woods, beach, river, etc.). You can keep the materials in a box or drawer or devote a corner of a room to your center. Here are some supplies I suggest for starting a nature center in your home:

- **Glass jars** or **plastic containers** of varying sizes for storing finds

- **Tape** and **marker** for labeling the containers

- A **magnifying glass**

- A **ruler** or **tape measure** for measuring natural treasures

- **Guidebooks** on nature, exploring, and identification

- A **small tray** or **plastic cutting board** to place objects on while studying them

- **Colored pencils** for sketching natural specimens

- **Notebook** for recording observations

IF YOU ARE SHORT ON SPACE OR NEED TO EDIT YOUR NATURE CENTER, HAVE YOUR CHILD DRAW THE FOUND ITEMS IN A NOTE-BOOK BEFORE DISCARDING THEM. THAT WAY, THEY CAN STILL REMEM-BER AND STUDY THE THING THEY FOUND, EVEN IF THEY DON'T HAVE THE PHYSICAL OBJECT ON HAND.

FIELD TIP

"We often come home with our pockets full of rocks, flowers, bark, moss, and anything else that strikes us while we are out walking. We then drop all our found items on our designated 'treasure' shelf. Rainy or cold days are the perfect times to check out those finds more closely. Maybe we look at them under a microscope or magnifying glass or try to identify them and find out more—the internet is full of resources for that kind of thing!"

—KATIE BOYLE is a forest school educator. She teaches Wonder Walks in Oxford, Mississippi, where she lives with her husband William and their two children. You can find Katie and her forest school students on Instagram: @wonderwalks.

TRY THIS:

Visiting National Parks and Protected Land

National parks are some of the most beautiful, wild places on Earth. They are like natural museums—you and your child can explore geology, history, environmental science, conservation, and so much more. They provide endless opportunities for learning and adventuring, whether you're taking a nature walk, swimming in a crystal clear lake, or planning a multiday camping trip. Spending time in protected land, whether on a state, national, or international level, is a great way to teach your child about protecting and caring for the natural world.

A WALK IN THE WOODS

Taking a short walk in nature is a great way to expose your child to the natural world and spend time together as a family. You don't have to take a difficult trail or climb a mountain—find a pace that works for your group and take your time. This is not about gaining a ton of elevation or covering a lot of distance—it's about listening to the birds, watching the clouds, touching bark, and gaining a respect for the creatures, plants, and ecosystems that make up our world. I recommend turning off your devices so that you and your child can really be present together in nature. Make sure to bring water and snacks, and wear clothes that can get dirty—in fact, getting a little dirty is encouraged! Here are some family activities for your next nature walk:

- **Listen for birds:** Take note of the bird-calls and, if possible, try to identify the birds behind each sound.

- **Look for animal tracks:** Find footprints and discuss which animal the tracks belong to. Sketch the tracks in a shared family journal.

- **Spend a moment in silence:** Find a place where everyone in your group can sit quietly. Have everyone close their eyes and make note of all the things that they hear in one minute. Record the sounds in a shared family journal.

- **Read a book:** Bring a favorite book and a blanket and have story time in the woods.

- **Look for webs:** Find a spiderweb and notice the designs created, without disturbing the web. Sketch the design in a shared journal.

- **Collect materials for a nature mobile:** Gather materials that have fallen on the ground, such as leaves, pinecones, sticks, and stones (don't remove anything that's still alive). Use twine to secure your found objects to a large stick.

- **Have an "I Spy" scavenger hunt:** Create a scavenger hunt and encourage your child to spot (not touch) things like squirrels, birds, acorns, berries, mushrooms, moss, and leaves. You can make it up as you go along or create a list before setting out on your adventure.

- **Look for birds' nests:** Search for birds' nests and discuss the tiny architects of the natural world. Remember, some birds build their nests on the ground, so always watch where you step.

- **Make a map:** Have your child draw a map of the path you took on the walk, making note of trees that you passed, streams crossed, big turns in the trail, and any other natural features you encountered. This will encourage your child to make note of their surroundings and develop a sense of direction.

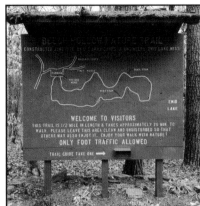

FIELD TIP

"I think it's important for kids (or anyone, really) to see that the places we learn about in books or in movies are actual places that take up space on this planet. They are places that can be touched, walked on, and experienced in real time. I think it makes those places more real or tangible. I want my children to know that the world is huge and diverse and that they exist in just a tiny portion of it. I want them to see that despite different environments, backgrounds, languages, and upbringings, people are all connected. That things are bigger than just them."

—ADRIENNE BROWN DAVID is a visual artist and homeschool teacher to two of her four daughters. She lives in Water Valley, Mississippi, with her husband Taariq and four daughters. You can follow Adrienne on Instagram: @adriennemeschelle.

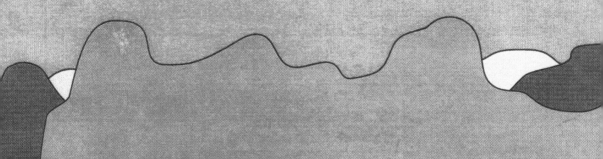

Traveling with Kids

Mapping Out Your Trips, Planning Tips, and More

In this section, you'll find entries on:

Getting Comfortable Traveling with Kids

Packing for a Family Trip

Making the Most of Each Location

Travel Tips for Planes, Cars, and Trains

Finding Inspiration in Everyday Places While You Travel

Traveling Off the Beaten Path

Capturing Your Adventures

Lesson Plans When Traveling

Preparing for a family trip is one of the things I love most about traveling. I love thinking of all the possibilities, researching activities, and figuring out what gear we'll need. But I've spoken with a lot of parents who are overwhelmed by travel *because* of the planning: deciding what to pack, planning kid-friendly activities, dealing with the cost of travel, and so on. I understand why traveling with kids can feel daunting, but I think what you gain from traveling with your children makes it all worth it. And if you're strategic, you can make the planning as fun as the trip itself! In this section I'll provide tips, resources, and activities that will hopefully alleviate some of the stress associated with traveling with kids so that you and your family can make wonderful travel memories.

Getting Comfortable Traveling with Kids

Whether you're planning an extended vacation abroad or a long weekend in the country, it's important to go at your own pace. There are many different types of travel styles, from slow travel where you take your time and wander with no concrete agenda, to action-packed adventures where you plan to do as much as possible in a short amount of time. It can be easy to get caught up by how other families plan their trips, but make sure you're creating a trip that feels comfortable for you and your family. Here are a few things to keep in mind as you start planning your trip.

- **Avoid high season if possible:** Your family will enjoy your trip so much more if you're not surrounded by tons of other tourists. Prices for hotels and flights often soar during peak season, so booking during the off-season can save you money. I realize it can be difficult to plan around your child's school schedule, so find out whether your child's school allows for travel during school days. Although my son is in a traditional school, I am allowed to take him out to travel with permission from the principal. Because travel can be so educational, his school is willing to work with parents to allow kids to miss classes and make up the missed schoolwork.

- **Make a map:** Once you have settled on your destination, start to make lists of places you'd like to try to work in. I tend to find more places than I could ever visit in one trip, but it just means that next time I return, I already have a list figured out of new places to see. Once you have

123

TRY THIS:

Black Friday Deals

Most airlines offer sales on Black Friday (the day after Thanksgiving). It's a good time to find great deals on flights.

your list, use an app like Google Maps to pin each location on your list. Before I started mapping out our travel activities, I'd realize later on that I'd been right around the corner from a shop I wanted to visit or a park I wanted to make sure to take Tom to, but didn't realize it because I didn't have the map sorted out. Mapping out your plans ahead of time will help you organize activities more strategically and allow you to see things you don't want to miss.

- **Don't try to pack it all in:** Don't feel pressured to see and do every single thing on your list. Pick a few places to see and give yourself time to really enjoy the experience. Remember that children can be easily exhausted or overwhelmed during travel, so taking a slower approach will ensure that everyone is happy and comfortable.

PLANNING A TRIP ABROAD

If you are traveling out of the country, there are some things you can do to make your life a whole lot easier before and during your trip:

- Make sure all passports and driver's licenses are up-to-date. Save yourself the headache that comes with trying to get these documents renewed at the last minute before your trip. Some countries require that your passport be at least six months old, so do your research before booking your travels.

- Check to see whether you're required to have a visa to enter the country you're planning to visit. Some places allow you to get visas when you enter the country, while others require that you apply for and obtain a visa ahead of time.

- Make a photocopy of each traveler's passport and store the copies in a safe place, separate from the physical passports.

- Make sure everyone in your party has the proper vaccinations for the country that you plan to visit. Some countries require proof of vaccination in order to enter the country.

- Find out whether you'll need a Child Travel Consent Form. If you are traveling out of the country with your child and the other parent is not traveling with you,

you will need a Child Travel Consent Form along with the child's passport. This form is a notarized letter from the other parent giving you permission to travel with your child. If you are a single parent without a co-parent, then a letter from the court might be required. While the United States does not always require this, many other countries do require these forms, so it's always better to err on the side of caution. (Be sure to check the country's embassy website for any additional requirements.)

- Call your cellphone company and set up an international plan. There's nothing more alarming than receiving an enormous phone bill because you didn't have the right international plan.

- Call your credit card companies and let them know where and when you'll be traveling so that they don't put a freeze on your card for unusual activity.

- Keep a list of your credit card numbers and your credit card company's international customer service phone numbers. Keep this information in a safe place, separate from your wallet. Having that information on hand makes things much easier if your card gets lost or stolen.

- Consider buying travel insurance to cover you in case you need to cancel or change your plans. You can tack it on to your flight when you book directly through the airlines.

Be Aware of Local Etiquette

When my mom and I planned a trip to India years and years ago, she reminded me that certain things were considered impolite there. I hadn't had much international travel at that point, so I wasn't as aware as I am now of the importance of following certain customs when you travel. These include what types of clothes to pack, what to be aware of in each location, and how to avoid offending locals.

Before you travel to a location, look up different things to be aware of with your child. Use this time to discuss the importance of cultural customs and traditions and how to be mindful of the country you are planning on visiting. You are a visitor in their country and it's important to be sensitive to their traditions rather than expecting them to cater to you. Here's a roundup of just a few country customs to keep in mind before visiting. There are many more, so prepare accordingly whenever you travel to a new country.

In India, you might be tempted to wear shorts, especially because temperatures can get so hot, but to respect religious customs, it's important to keep the lower part of your body covered.

FIELD TIP

"Find what works best for your family and ways to engage your children that they will respond well to. We often expose our children to a city through eating. In San Francisco, we get our favorite Thai and Vietnamese food and burritos in the Mission. We have a big sushi lover in the family, so we find a place for that, too. Walking around each city is and always has been our way of discovering, and we still do this with the kids. Our oldest likes to see where we are headed and what's around. Our middle daughter likes the cultural part of traveling—the people, the music. She's happy just wandering, with no plan, just people watching and seeing shows and bands play."

—KORI GARDNER is a music teacher, songwriter, and member of the indie band Mates of State, which she started with her husband Jason. She lives in Connecticut with her husband and three children.

In Brazil, food is rarely eaten with the hands. So when in doubt, use a fork and knife for everything.

In Spain, a late lunch is the big meal, with three or four courses. Dinner is often eaten around 10 p.m. This doesn't mean you need to adhere to that, but don't be surprised if you are one of the only ones in a restaurant. This might be a good time to have a picnic dinner instead.

In Japan, tipping is considered rude. And bow when you greet someone. Bowing is like saying hi.

In England, make sure to have your "pleases" and "thank yous" ready. It's highly expected to say it any chance you get.

In Thailand, you eat food with a spoon. Don't assume because it's an Asian culture that they use chopsticks.

In Tanzania, many of the citizens are Muslim, and covering up respectfully is common. A head covering is not required, but do dress modestly.

In Indonesia, if you need to point, use your right thumb. Using your index finger is considered rude. Also, treat everyone you meet like you are a guest in their home. Politeness is key here.

In France, it's common to see people cut in line. If someone jumps in front of you, rather than getting upset, it's best to brush it off.

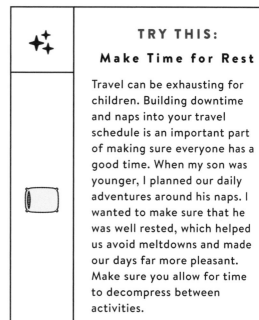

TRY THIS:

Make Time for Rest

Travel can be exhausting for children. Building downtime and naps into your travel schedule is an important part of making sure everyone has a good time. When my son was younger, I planned our daily adventures around his naps. I wanted to make sure that he was well rested, which helped us avoid meltdowns and made our days far more pleasant. Make sure you allow for time to decompress between activities.

PLANNING A ROAD TRIP

Whenever we're planning a family road trip, I always try to do certain tasks ahead of time, which helps things go smoothly when we're actually on the road:

- **Do a vehicle check:** If you're planning to take your own car, make sure it is fully serviced and detailed before leaving. Check to make sure you have your insurance and roadside assistance numbers on hand, and that your spare tire is in good condition in case you need to use it. Knowing that your car is in working order before your trip will give you peace of mind and hopefully avoid any unfortunate car issues along the way.

- **Plan for stops along the way:** Make sure your itinerary leaves plenty of time for breaks to stretch, move around, and use the bathroom. Getting out of the car every once in a while will make the trip far more enjoyable for everyone. Do a little bit of research ahead of time to find fun places to pull over to break up the drive, like roadside attractions and local diners.

- **Book your accommodations ahead of time:** Plan your hotel locations ahead of time rather than showing up in a new location and hoping to find a hotel. You might end up having to pay a little more by booking ahead of time (versus finding a cheaper place to stay when you arrive), but it's better than having to drive an extra 100 miles when you are tired because you couldn't find a vacant room.

TRY THIS:

Save Money on Road Trip Accommodations

Consider booking most of your en route accommodations through the same family of hotels so that you can accumulate points toward free stays. If you want to stay at a boutique hotel that's more expensive, I recommend saving that for your final destination rather than while you're on the road so you can make the most of your stay. If you're staying in a place for more than a few nights, look for a hotel or a rented residential apartment with a refrigerator or full kitchen, so that you can get a few staples at the grocery store, save money on meals, and keep leftovers from dining out.

TRY THIS:

Car Essentials

Here are a few things to keep in the car during family road trips:

- A first aid kit: Include adhesive and elastic bandages, allergy medicine, scissors, and anything else you think you might need.

- A spare set of car keys: Losing your only set of keys on a road trip is no fun. Some car manufacturers charge as much as $700 for a replacement key, which could really put a dent in your travel budget.

- A five-port car charger and charging cords: Multi-port chargers allow everyone to charge their devices at the same time.

FIELD TIP

"If your children say they want to nap instead of seeing the Eiffel Tower, trust them and leave it for another day. Keep expectations low for the amount you can see in a day— always work in time for a nap or quiet time."

—AMANDA JANE JONES is a graphic designer and mother to two children. She and her husband Cree are coauthors of the children's book *Yum, Yummy, Yuck*. You can find Amanda on Instagram: @AmandaJaneJones.

Packing for a Family Trip

Packing for a trip can be daunting and overwhelming, but I'm here to tell you, it doesn't have to be. Here are some tips I've found to be helpful when we're packing for a family trip:

- **Start packing several days before your trip:** This gives you time to think and rethink what you are taking and adjust your bag accordingly. Instead of throwing everything together the night before your trip, packing ahead of time provides a few days to edit your bag and takes some of the stress out of last-minute packing. You won't have to look for items that have gone missing or run to the store for an item at the last minute.

- **If traveling by airplane, plan to check most of your bags:** I recommend that each person bring a small carry-on and check everything else. I do this with my own family because in my experience it's just too difficult to navigate busy airports and crowded airplanes with all our luggage.

- **Wear what you know:** Don't be tempted to buy a bunch of new clothes for a trip. Instead, I recommend packing

tried-and-true items that you and your children wear on a regular basis. That way, you know everyone will be comfortable on your travels, rather than regretting a new purchase that doesn't fit right or having to break in a new pair of shoes.

TRY THIS:

Bring a Portable Speaker

White noise can help block out street sounds or noises from nearby hotel rooms that might keep your child awake during your travels. When our son was younger we traveled with a very small Bluetooth speaker that we could use to play white noise, or we called ahead to ask if the hotel had one we could use.

The DREAM CATCHER

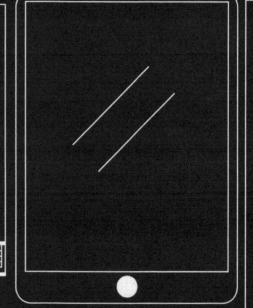

E. N. Greene

ALMONDS

TRY THIS:

Pack a Cooler

If this is a car trip or you plan to rent a car at your final destination and do a lot of driving, consider bringing a collapsible insulated cooler bag. This will allow you to stock up on easy, healthy snacks for your drives, like carrots, hummus, cheese, and cold water (having snacks on hand has saved our son from many road trip meltdowns). You can also purchase a cooler at a grocery store or shopping center when you arrive at your location.

- **Bring multiuse items that can be layered:** Pack items that can be worn to a variety of places. For example, I pick things like dark jeans, a dark-colored button-up top with a T-shirt underneath, and a cardigan that I can wear from the museum to the park to a restaurant for dinner. I also recommend packing items that you can layer so that you don't have to pack bulky jackets, which take up a lot of room and you may not end up needing (though of course if you're traveling to a cold place, bring warm coats!).

- **Think about packing in a color palette,** like all gray, black, and white, so that it's easy to mix and match your pieces without clashing.

- **Stick with darker-colored clothing:** Darker clothes make it easy to hide little stains that you might not be able to tend to right away when traveling.

- **Color code:** Organize your belongings into small, color-coded packing cubes and assign a color to each member of your family. These simple cubes make for easier packing and unpacking so you don't have to rifle through everyone's belongings every time you're trying to find something.

- **Consider whether you'll have access to laundry:** You can pack a lot less if you know you'll have access to laundry. You can do laundry almost anywhere, whether it's at a local Laundromat, at your rental home, or through your hotel's laundry service or a drop-off service (in New York City we used a service that washed, folded, and pressed all our laundry). Laundromats can provide a great opportunity for a field trip to an everyday place with your child (see page 160). My son and I have had some great conversations with locals at Laundromats we've used on our travels.

Packing the Carry-On Bag

Must-haves for the carry-on when you're traveling with kids:

☐ **All electronics and chargers**

☐ **Important documents in waterproof bag**

☐ **Headphones**

☐ **Quiet game such as travel checkers or a deck of cards**

☐ **Reading materials**

☐ **Snacks**

☐ **Map of destination**

☐ **Very small toiletry bag with allergy tablets (rather than a bulky liquid form), a few plastic sandwich bags, child and adult ibuprofen, and adhesive bandages**

- **Don't bring the kitchen sink:** Packing for children can feel like you are packing enough belongings to clothe and entertain a small town. Consider whether you can pick up some of the things you need at your final destination, and remember that you can usually buy essential supplies like diapers, shampoo, snacks, and even toys in most locations.

- **Ask your child to participate in the packing process:** This will help them envision the upcoming trip and give them a chance to ask questions about the place you're visiting. And if they get to help decide what to pack, it's more likely that they'll be happy with the outfits, toys, and supplies you bring. This will also help them become better planners and packers so that they can eventually pack for themselves, without your help.

TRY THIS:

Things You Didn't Know You Could Ask for During a Hotel Stay

Phone chargers: If you forgot a charger, your hotel front desk often has one you can borrow.

Pillows: Are you particular about the pillow you use? Many hotels can accommodate requests for firm, medium, or soft pillows.

Cribs: Many hotels can provide a crib or a pack 'n play for your child, so call ahead to see whether you can save yourself the headache of bringing your own from home. I would recommend bringing your own sheet for your child.

Gym time: Looking to get an extra workout in, but your hotel doesn't have a gym? Some hotels have a partnership with a local gym to allow you to get a very reduced day pass, or they even have yoga mats that you can borrow. Some also have workout gear you can borrow.

Car service: Ask whether they offer a complimentary car service. Some hotels have cars you can borrow or a car service that is provided by the hotel.

Toiletries: If you forgot a few basic toiletries like a toothbrush or toothpaste, just check with the front desk to see whether they have any of these to offer before running out to look for a drugstore.

Children's books and toys: Books and toys, such as bath toys, are often available by request. Call ahead to see whether your hotel can provide these things so you can save space in your luggage.

High chairs: A high chair is sometimes available. If not, we always used to put our son in his stroller to eat. He'd be contained and we'd pull him up to a small table to eat. We would also lay out a towel on the hotel floor and let him have a picnic.

Quick snacks: If you need a quick and easy snack for you or your child, many hotels will provide apples and bananas at no extra charge.

FIELD TIP

"We gave up packing our own car seats when we travel. Instead, we just order them online and have them shipped to arrive at the hotel the day before we get there. This costs less than renting one through the rental agencies, saves us the headache of not knowing whether they'll have the right sizes, and allows us to donate them when we are finished. We have been able to connect with young families, local schools, and other people who are more than happy to acquire some new car seats, and it's fun for our kids to think about who may now be riding in their seats."

—LAUREN BRYAN KNIGHT lives in London with her husband and their three children. She is the founder of the blog *Aspiring Kennedy*, which offers a look into her European travels and provides opportunities for group adventures. You can find Lauren on Instagram: @aspiringkennedy.

Making the Most of Each Location

Something I hear from a lot of friends who have just returned from a family trip is "I just wish we'd had more time to do _____." Let this section be your guide to planning trips where you're making the most of your time—whether that means leisurely days or an action-packed adventure. Here you'll find tips to help you plan your trip so that you can enjoy each moment of your journey and get the most out of your travels (without feeling stressed!).

VISITING A BIG CITY

Traveling in a city doesn't have to be overwhelming. Do some research ahead of time to figure out a plan for how you'll get around and whether you need to book certain activities—like shows, museum passes, or landmark visits—ahead of time. If you're renting a home, ask your host for local recommendations that are child-friendly; if you're staying at a hotel, speak with someone at the front desk. Here are some tips for making the most of your city visit:

- Visit one or two small art galleries around the city and ask to speak with the curator about the current exhibit. Ask how the work was selected, more information about the artist, and how they go about picking the work for each show. Encourage your child to keep this visit as part of their travel journals (page 176). You could do the same for interviewing chefs.

- Wander through a farmers' market, looking for food that either you or your children have never tried. Make guesses as to what it tastes like, writing it all down. Look up the food when you have a chance, try it if you spot it on a menu, or recreate recipes when you return home from your travels.

- Count how many public works you can find.

- Look for street musicians and enjoy a mini concert.

- Hop on a city bus and let it take you on a sightseeing journey.

- Find a classic movie theater and see a movie.

VISITING A SMALL TOWN

I love the slow pace that comes from visiting small towns. Small towns provide opportunities to shop in local, family-owned stores, eat in small restaurants that serve regional cuisine, and connect with residents in meaningful ways. You visit a small town for the slower pace of travel, so embrace it! Here are a few ideas to get you started on your next family trip to a small town:

- Stop by the local tourism bureau for maps and travel insight.

- Wander down the main street and chat with local shopkeepers.

- Rent bikes to get around town.

- Visit a local artist's studio.

- Head to the local library or bookstore for story time.

- Look up community theater productions and take in a play.

- Find the local historic spots to visit, like a famous artist's home.

VISITING RURAL AREAS AND MOUNTAIN TOWNS

I love visiting rural areas—taking winding roads, peering through the trees to spot the occasional house or small town. When we're traveling to a rural place, we try to make time to stop at scenic overlooks, plan a picnic with a view, and take a child-friendly hike. These trips provide wonderful opportunities for slowing down and enjoying the great outdoors. Here are a few activities to consider for your next rural adventure:

- Find a creek and race dead leaves downstream.

- Go bird-watching.

- Rent a canoe or kayak and paddle down a river.

- Build a fire and roast marshmallows.

- Rent fishing poles and spend an afternoon fishing.

- Go on a nature walk.

- Pick wild blueberries.

- Take a gondola or chairlift to the top of a ski mountain.

FIELD TIP

"When we are in a new place with our two children, our main way that we encourage our children to explore off the beaten path and see new things is by walking. Wherever we go, we try to walk as much as possible. We always find better or more interesting things to do when we walk. We live in Oklahoma City, which can be kind of insulated sometimes. So we hope that when we travel our kids get to see that people have different ways of living and different ways of being in communities. Walking in new places helps with that."

— STEVEN DROZD is a founding member of the band The Flaming Lips. When not on tour with the band, he lives in Oklahoma City with his wife Becky and their two children. You can find Steven on Instagram: @stevendrozd.

FIELD TIP

"We take a fairly laid-back approach to traveling with our children, and don't follow much of an itinerary. As long as we know where we'll be sleeping, anything goes! We almost always follow the local lead. I also find children are the best tour guides imaginable. They know how to pay attention to their surroundings; they know how to find newness and uncover beauty. In London, we set out to visit a butterfly museum exhibit that I was sure would fascinate and delight my toddler daughter. But she instead became enamored with a street performer's fiddle, so we enjoyed a lovely afternoon concert instead. We keep our minds and days open. We observe and ask questions. Mostly, we refuse to rush the process with checklists and itineraries, must-sees or must-dos."

—ERIN LOECHNER is the author of *Chasing Slow* and founder of OtherGoose.com, a home-schooling community. Based in Kansas, she has traveled the world with her husband Ken and two children. You can find her on Instagram: @Erinloechner.

VISITING A BEACH TOWN

The beach is a natural wonderland for learning. You can look for shells, build a sandcastle, gather clams, write notes in the sand, go for long beach walks, plan a treasure hunt, walk out to a sandbar, look for tide pools, and watch for dolphins or whales. If you're looking for some time away from the sand and water, here are a few ideas for beach town activities:

- Visit the local port and watch boats coming and going.

- Rent bikes and pedal around town.

- Visit the maritime museum.

- Visit local art galleries.

- Walk the boardwalk.

- Eat at seafood restaurants serving the catch of the day.

- Attend a local film or food festival.

FIELD TIP

"Playing games, taking walks, cooking and reading at home, eating at little cafes and restaurants, going to the park, and just being together in a space with so few distractions can create the perfect environment for meaningful time together. Rural areas where choices are limited generally lend themselves to a lot of quiet time together and less decision fatigue. When we stayed in a little town in the Cotswolds in England, we would meander to the local bakery in the morning. We'd bring our hot cross buns to the park after, where my children would play with local children as if they were real neighbors. Then we'd make our way to an old abbey that was over a thousand years old. There were no lines there and generally only one or two people. We would observe all of the little details of the church, talking all along the way, comparing it to other churches we'd seen, and imagining how people lived then and the stories that took place there. When you think about how much information is being taken in just in those three small experiences, it's pretty incredible."

—ELLE ROWLEY is the founder of Solly Baby Wrap. She lives with her husband Jared and their four children in Southern California. You can find Elle on Instagram: @Ellerowley.

"We always venture to places off the beaten path. We prefer finding locally loved eateries and beaches that are quiet, far from the tourist spots. We've also done a lot of road trips to smaller cities that are within a day's drive, even if they aren't typical vacation destinations. Our feeling is that we can have a great time exploring anywhere, and those places are often the most accessible and affordable."

—SARAH FORTUNE GILL lives in Fayetteville, Arkansas, with her husband Todd and their daughter. She travels often and shares her family's adventures through her blog at sarahfortune.com and on Instagram: @Sarahfortune.

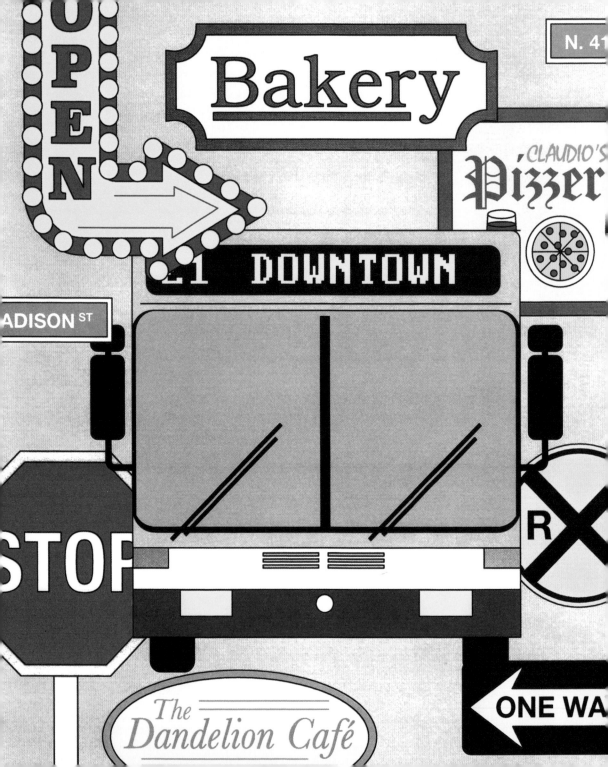

Travel Tips for Planes, Cars, and Trains

Even the most experienced parents don't know what to expect from their children when it comes to how a travel day will go. It's always unpredictable, but if you have a few supplies on hand and ideas to redirect their attention and keep them entertained you'll be as prepared as possible! In this section, you'll find suggestions for different forms of travel, including supplies to pack, and some jumping-off points when you need an activity suggestion for your children.

PLANE TRAVEL

Before You Go:

- Teach children to use their "airplane voice" so that you don't disturb the other passengers on the plane. Practice for about a week before your flight.

- Make sure you and your children drink lots of water, before you leave and once in flight. Bring a water bottle that you can fill at the airport once you get through security so that you don't have to wait for the service cart to come through the plane.

- Request seats in the back of the plane. People watching is entertaining for children and the hum of the plane works like white noise if they get a little rowdy. If you are traveling alone with your child, you are close to the bathroom and flight attendants at the back of the plane generally don't mind helping you with your child for a few minutes if you need to use the restroom.

- Talk to your child about respect for the people around you on the plane and what that looks like. Use examples that they understand, like how you share at the playground, sometimes with children that you've never met.

- For younger children, making a necklace of Cheerios ahead of time for them to wear and eat once on the plane helps in a pinch if your child is getting fussy.

Activities for Plane Travel:

- **Pipe cleaner statues:** Make pipe cleaner designs with your child during the flight.

- **Tape art:** Make designs on the tray table with masking or washi tape. It peels right off as you begin your descent.

- **Little presents:** Prewrap a few small objects—like a new eraser, or a sheet of stickers—and present them to your child throughout the flight.

- **Map play:** Bring a map of the location you're visiting and share it with your child. It's a great way to prepare them for what to expect once you land. Talk about the routes you will take and let them trace the route in a journal or on a piece of paper.

- **Play-Doh:** Bring several of the small containers of Play-Doh and let your children get creative.

- **Magnetic blocks:** Tegu makes a travel set—and what better time to try it out! The magnets keep their structures contained and prevent children from losing little pieces beneath their seat.

- **Cloud spotting:** If you have a window seat, encourage your child to look for clouds in the shape of recognizable animals, people, or objects.

- **Puppet theater:** Bring finger puppets or sock puppets and put on a play with your child.

- **Journaling:** Bring a notebook or journal, such as a travel journal (page 176), and give your child time to draw or write in it.

FIELD TIP

"When we travel by plane, we always bring blankets to help the kids feel more cozy. We love bringing lots of stickers and tape and new activities. For our trip to South Africa, we went to the dollar store and wrapped up a whole bunch of little activities and toys in foil. Every hour they got a new one! It worked great and helped pass the time."

—AMANDA JANE JONES is a graphic designer and mother to two children. She and her husband Cree are coauthors of the children's book *Yum, Yummy, Yuck*. You can find Amanda on Instagram: @AmandaJaneJones.

CAR TRAVEL

Before You Go:

- Get each child their own set of earphones to use on an iPod or iPad. If you only have one device, get an earphone splitter, so they have their own earphones.

- Create playlists for the road, including quiet songs, dance songs, and sing-along songs. Let your child contribute suggestions.

- Install over-the-seat organizers. These inventions hang over car seats and are great for storing all the little things kids need on a trip, like water bottles, paper and crayons, favorite stuffed animals for naps, eye masks if they are sensitive to light when sleeping in the car, disposable cameras, small toys, maps, and more.

- Give your children seat belt pillows (cushions that attach over the seat belt), so you don't have to pack a large one from home.

- Make bingo cards with things you might see along the route.

- Create a LEGO box using a metal lunchbox. Glue the main LEGO building board to the inside of the tin and let them build inside the box. They can store all the pieces inside the box when they're finished.

Activities for Road Travel:

- **Pit stops:** Look for rest stops with a picnic area so your child can run around for a little bit. Pack a lunch or look up good local restaurants you'll pass on your drive and call in a to-go order.

- **Roadtrip bingo:** Give each passenger a bingo card and fill them out throughout the drive.

- **Learn a language:** Bring audio materials for learning a new language. Road trips are a great time for the whole family to practice a foreign language.

- **Story time:** Audiobooks are a great road trip activity. A long trip is the perfect time to start a series like Harry Potter.

- **Play the "Finish Game":** One person starts a story or drawing and you each work to add to it and collaboratively finish it.

- **Practice navigation skills:** Put your destination into a GPS and ask your children to help you navigate. Encourage them to keep a lookout for turns, and use this time to talk about coordinates and cardinal directions (page 68).

- **Multiple-path adventure story:** Encourage older childen to write a design-your-own-adventure story on the drive, incorporating places and objects they see out the window.

TRY THIS:

Tackling Time Zones and Scheduling When Away from Home

Changing time zones can be really difficult on children. I've heard so many parents talk about their child waking up at 3 a.m. on a trip and not going back to sleep for hours. The best trick I learned from my travel nanny years, after many trips around the world with children, is to acclimate children to the local time as quickly as possible. Coordinate flights and time zones as best you can to avoid disturbing their regular sleeping routine. For example, my son goes to bed at 6:30 p.m. Mississippi time, and say we are going to France, which is six hours ahead of us. I would look for flights that left in the afternoon and arrived in France the next morning. I'd encourage him to sleep on the airplane, dressing him in comfortable clothes that he can sleep in, read him a bedtime story, and have him brush his teeth on the plane so that it feels like our normal bedtime routine. Once we arrived, I would keep my son up until his normal bedtime of 6:30 p.m. Paris time. This would help quickly acclimate him to the local time.

FIELD TIP

"I think my daughters bond more when we travel. When they are in a new place, surrounded by different people, they are compelled to look to each other for a sense of home. They have so many memories and funny stories about trips we've taken and places that we've visited, and they'll have those memories forever. I usually have the kids map out the route on a paper map and then Google cool stops along the way. They've discovered some pretty amazing stops for us on those trips."

—ADRIENNE BROWN DAVID is a visual artist and homeschool teacher to two of her four daughters. She lives in Water Valley, Mississippi, with her husband Taariq and four daughters. You can follow Adrienne on Instagram: @adriennemeschelle.

TRAIN TRAVEL

Train Tips:

When you're booking tickets, be sure to look for kids' fares, which are often a good deal cheaper than adult fares. Sometimes children can even travel for free!

Arrive at least thirty minutes before departure so you don't feel rushed. Use this time to show your child the arrival and departure boards. For a learning lesson, talk to them about the distance between cities and show them the different cities on a map.

When you board the train, look for seats with a table so your kids have a surface to eat and play on. If you can afford to pay a little more, you can sometimes get your own cabin, too, which means you have a quiet space and room to spread out.

Activities for Train Travel:

- **What do you spot?:** Traveling by train is a great opportunity for endless observation. Encourage your child to do some travel journaling (page 176) while on the train. Have them journal or draw the things they see along the way, like towns, streams, clouds, tunnels, and trees.

- **Train zen:** Trains can sometimes require a bit more patience. Use this time to do a five-minute meditation with your child. Teach the importance of daydreaming, finding calm, and learning about stillness. Afterward, reflect together on what you felt in those minutes and encourage your child to write it down in their travel journal.

- **Listening time:** On a longer trip, this is a good time to listen to an audiobook or learn a language together. Use a headphone splitter to listen together and then talk about the story or review the language lesson afterward.

- **Take a walk:** Many trains allow you to walk between cars. If you're on a long train ride, take your child for a walk through the train so they can stretch their legs and get out of their seat for a bit.

OUTSIDE
THE
LINES

RTA ▶▶

ST. CHARLES — 01

903

HOW'S MY DRIVING
CALL 248-3900

Please Have Exact Fare
Or RTA Pass Ready

Finding Inspiration in Everyday Places While You Travel

When we travel as a family, we love stopping at places that are central to everyday life—like grocery stores, post offices, and subway stations—and picking up little souvenirs. Spending time at places like a grocery store may seem mundane, but these kinds of errands allow children to see what day-to-day life is like in a new place, whether it's a different state or a foreign country, and that it isn't all that different from their life at home. Observing these similarities will help them broaden their global perspective. This observation practice helps children see the similarities between various cultures and ways of living, rather than viewing new experiences as "other." And being comfortable in new places will help them learn to adapt to different situations quickly, which could mean fewer meltdowns and more problem-solving on their part.

Here are a few examples of everyday places to look for on your travels:

Street Markets

When you're traveling, look for open-air markets, farmers' markets or stands, and small flea markets. These markets tell you so much about a place; often they are the heart of a town or city. They are where chefs select fresh ingredients, where families go to feed and clothe their children, where artists sell their original work. Visiting these markets will give your child a chance to see how locals live, eat, work, and shop, which will give them a wonderful sense of place that they can't get from only visiting tourist sites.

Gas Stations

This might seem like a strange suggestion, but gas stations can be a fantastic place to visit. Look for stations that are different from the ones that you see at home—maybe they have different architecture, or the pumping stations look unfamiliar. And you never know when you might stumble upon a gas station that serves delicious food—in Mississippi, where I live, you can get amazing tamales, muffuletta sandwiches, Indian food, BBQ, and soul food, all at gas stations. Some of the most authentic food can sometimes be found in gas stations.

Post Offices

I love to find post offices when I travel. They are often housed in old buildings with lots of character and charm, and they have one of the most wonderful, inexpensive souvenirs— postage stamps. Stamps reveal so much about a place, from landscape to culture to history, and they are a great way to jazz up your correspondence. Even if you're staying close to home, the post office is a great place to take your child to learn about how the postal system works.

Grocery Stores

Grocery stores allow you to explore a variety of produce that you and your child might not see in your own local store. Wander down the fruit and vegetable aisles and see whether you can pick out some items that are hard to find where you live. Grocery stores are also a great place to talk about economics and currency, especially if you are in a foreign country. Noticing prices helps children become money wise early in their lives. Grocery stores can help you navigate a new place: If you're traveling in a foreign country, stop into grocery stores to make note of the words for different foods—for example, you can figure out the word for "rice" by finding a bag of rice and reading the label or the word for "milk" by looking at a carton of milk. Keep a running list of the words you've learned so that you can order off menus confidently.

If you are staying close to home, find an international market in your area and browse the aisles with your child, looking for new spices, ingredients, or snacks to try.

Public Transportation

When I was a travel nanny, I would take the children on a train or subway any chance we got, even if we were just going to loop back to where we came from. Public transportation provides so many great lessons and is an inexpensive way to tour a new place. Public transportation stations, like bus terminals and subway stations, can also be great places for children to learn about navigation. Learning the artery of a city and understanding basic forms of transportation are vital to becoming a traveler. And surrounding yourself with locals, commuters, and the like is a great way to become a citizen of the world.

Playgrounds

We love visiting playgrounds when we travel. When children are far away from home, playing on a local, neighborhood playground provides them with an opportunity to meet other kids and learn new games they might not be exposed to back home. Do a little research ahead of time to find out whether the location you are visiting has a unique playground to visit. Plan to go at a time when it's likely other children will be there—like after school or on a weekend. Encourage your child to make a new friend or learn a new game with the other kids at the park. This is an excellent chance for them to interact with children from other places, which will help broaden your child's understanding of the world around them. They might even learn a new word or find a pen pal!

Traveling Off the Beaten Path

Sometimes we return home from a trip and hear about a spot that we wish we'd visited on our travels. It could be that we walked right by an incredible hole-in-the-wall bookstore or drove by the trail to a world-famous waterfall because we didn't know to look for it. Here are some wonderful resources that will help you find the not-to-miss spots at your destination:

- **Geotags:** Because of social media and geotags, we can now see the beauty of a location from every traveler who has "geotagged" their location. Geotags allow you to see where people visit, including hotels, playgrounds, restaurants, shops, and so on. Look for geotags on sites like Instagram, Pinterest, Facebook, Snapchat, and YouTube. If you are geotagging a place of natural beauty, consider giving it a general tag of the nearby town or park rather than the specific site so that it doesn't become too overrun or trampled. We want to encourage children to care for these natural wonders rather than add to their demise, which can happen when a place is overshared.

- **Pinterest:** Pinterest is a great tool for planning your entire trip in one location. Create a board for your trip and fill it with places to visit: restaurants, playgrounds, museums, shops, artist studios, public transportation maps, street maps, packing lists, and helpful words and phrases. All the information will be accessible on your phone, via the Pinterest app, while you travel.

- **Blogs:** When a blogger writes about a city or a place to visit, they will either give you a firsthand account of their experience or ask a local to write the feature. Try reachinging out to a blogger directly if you have questions or would like some updated suggestions. Many bloggers love to connect with their readers and would be happy to offer some help.

- **Airbnb:** Airbnb provides suggestions for experiences, such as hiring a local to take a cultural walk through a food market, booking a bike tour, learning to play an instrument, or taking a surfing lesson.

- **Travel shows:** Online streaming services provide a plethora of amazing travel shows that offer plenty of inspiration for locations to visit, restaurants to try, and cultural events to attend.

- **Magazine websites:** Many magazines post extra content on their websites that take you deeper than what they print. You can search by city, food type, country, etc.

FIELD TIP

"Don't be afraid to travel with kids when they are small and the airfare is free! Traveling with my daughter Iris at a young age has helped her become an amazing travel companion. I just wish we had taken more advantage of the free airfare when she was under two years old."

—SARAH FORTUNE GILL lives in Fayetteville, Arkansas, with her husband Todd and their daughter. She travels often and shares her family's adventures through her blog at sarahfortune. com and on Instagram: @Sarahfortune.

FIELD TIP

"When we visited Beijing, China, years ago, we first walked along one of the most prominent shopping streets in the city, which has amazing state-of-the-art shopping malls, fancy restaurants, and hotels. And then, instead of walking the same way back, we decided to walk along a smaller street, which is just parallel to the shopping street, and we were shocked with what we saw. People there were living in tiny rooms with shared public toilets. They had no private telephone at home, but shared one on the street. That was an eye-opener for all of us, and it taught us to look beyond the surface. Since then, every time when we travel, we walk and drive around in less popular and touristy areas to see what life is like for the locals."

—MADELINE LU is a photographer and global wanderer who lives in San Francisco, California, with her husband and two kids. Madeline and her family have traveled to more than thirty countries and counting. You can follow her travels on Instagram: @lumadeline.

Capturing Your Adventures

When I was a little girl, my mom always had a camera around her neck and was often busy jotting down memories from our adventures in her journal. Now that I'm a parent I model this same behavior for my son. Teaching children to document their adventures will give them a lasting artifact to remind them of their travels. They can write about the sounds and smells of a new place, sketch a structure, or write about the friend they met at the playground. The easy-to-follow ideas in this section will encourage your child to capture their experiences so that they can reflect on happy memories and exciting adventures for many years to come.

GIVING YOUR CHILD A CAMERA

Allowing children to partake in documenting their journey makes them more active and curious observers, and seeing the trip through your children's eyes is such a special experience. I recommend buying a disposable camera or an inexpensive digital one, and doing a short lesson on camera care and storage. Then let them be free to take pictures of whatever they want. The point is that they get to choose what they want to capture. Ask them about what they are shooting and ask why it drew their attention. It's not about expecting masterful works of art, but rather about getting them familiar with seeing the world around them in a different way. Encourage your budding artist to notice small details and find the beauty all around them.

We started my son out with a disposable camera when he was just about two years old.

Were the pictures great then? No, not by a long shot! But that wasn't the point—giving him a camera at a young age helped him be more observant, gave him a chance to learn about how cameras work, and provided an opportunity for him to practice taking care of a camera while we traveled. Eventually, I gave him my old digital camera. We talk about how to care for it and how special it is, and he has to use the neck strap whenever he's taking photos.

KEEPING A TRAVEL JOURNAL

Travel journals are a wonderful way to record memories and make for special mementos to look back on once you've returned from your trips. You can either encourage your child to keep their own travel journal or you can keep a shared family travel journal, where you all work together to record your adventures. I recommend getting a small journal for each trip you take. When you return home, store the travel journal with journals from past travels to make a little travel library that you can revisit as a family.

Ideas to record in your journal:

- Draw maps of places you visit.

- Write down where you go, the types of things you hear in each location, and what you see.

- Record favorite meals and restaurants, and keep a list of any new foods you try.

- Write down funny things that were said.

- Make a list of places that you'd want to return to or places that you ran out of time to see.

- Draw observations of the natural world, including birds, trees, leaves, etc.

- Draw the sunset, along with the date, time, and place.

- Tape ticket stubs and small mementos into the journal.

COLLECTING TRAVEL SOUVENIRS

Souvenirs have a reputation for being tacky, but they can also be fun, inexpensive reminders of the places you've traveled with your family. We collect everything from pressed pennies to restaurant menus to maps of places we visit, and we've come up with some creative ways to display our collection. Here are a few ideas for things to collect and how to show off your souvenirs:

- **Snow globes:** Scatter them throughout a bookshelf, resting them between and on top of stacks of books. You can also fill the top of a dresser with a bunch of snow globes, creating a large, visual display. If you do pick up snow globes on your travels, be sure to let the water out so it doesn't spill in transit.

- **Pressed pennies:** Keep your pressed pennies in a jar. Spread them out on the floor from time to time and talk about each location and your adventures there.

- **Patches:** Patches can be sewn or ironed on to a jacket or a favorite backpack. Or you can place them in small frames and hang them to create a gallery wall of memories.

- **Natural objects:** Gather bits of found nature that have already dropped to the ground—such as leaves, small stones, and shells (I don't encourage removing living nature, such as leaves from trees)—and keep them in a glass jar, labeled with the date and place on the lid. This will serve as a sort of visual travel diary. Know the rules of the place you are traveling. Some locations don't allow you to remove things like shells or flowers. If that's the case, encourage children to snap a picture of the found object or create a drawing for their nature journal.

- **Travel box**: Create small travel boxes for each of your trips. Fill them with mementos, and then label each one with the name of the place you visited. Store the boxes on a bookshelf with the labels visible or place them in your travel center (see page 32).

FIELD TIP

"My kids see me shoot photos informally all the time—I take photos on family trips constantly and also more formally on occasion; they have spent entire days on big sets with me where they can gain an understanding of the production aspects that go into a shoot. I really don't speak to them about the technical aspects of cameras or anything like that, but I do like to point out when I see pretty light, or just pretty things that would make for a nice photo. I hope that by using this more hands-off approach, they can choose to follow whatever path they'd like to—whether they do something creative in the future or not—and that that appreciation for beauty and art will affect whatever it is they do in life."

— CHRIS OZER is a professional photographer living in Brooklyn, New York, with his wife Erin and their two boys. You can find Chris on Instagram: @chrisozer.

FIELD TIP

"We love bringing home mementos from our travels, and they are sprinkled throughout our home. The children's dad usually travels a lot out of the country for work, and I was inspired to install a map mural in the boys' room so they could 'see' the places he travels to and get an idea of where in the world these places are. Now, if their dad is going overseas, he'll show the boys where he is going on the map mural and tell them a bit about the place. The children enjoy being able to identify where in the world these places are, and it helps them better envision their dad's experiences."

—STACEY BLAKE is the founder of the blog *Design Addict Mom*, where she showcases her design work and shares the latest in design news and trends. She lives in North Carolina with her husband and three children. You can find Stacey on Instagram: @designaddictmom.

Lesson Plans When Traveling

When you are traveling, whether for a short family vacation or longer international trips, I recommend coming up with a few easy lessons and activities that will keep your child engaged in the travel experience. For example, consider planning a fun scavenger hunt when you're visiting a museum or planning a walk to study the architecture in a city. Giving children things to look for, record, and discuss is a great way to keep them excited and interested in exploring a new place.

I also recommend doing a little bit of research ahead of time to look into local events in the place you're visiting. If you are in a university town, check out the campus website to see whether the science department is having an event or a campus group is putting on an international dance performance. If you're visiting a city, peruse the local paper to find a wealth of listings for fun family events—local art shows, concerts for kids, dance performances, summer theater, small playhouses, pop-up restaurants, markets, and more. The ideas are endless if you just know where to look. Over the next few pages, you'll find a sample lesson plan and some approachable activities that you can incorporate into your travels.

HOW TO CREATE LESSON PLANS AWAY FROM HOME

Once you've done some research about where you're going, you can start planning your lessons. For a more formal approach to learning, build from the following format, as discussed in Section One (pages 26–31): Topic, Objective and goals, Supply list, Guided instruction, Guided activity, and a reading list. This format

FIELD TIP

"'It's an adventure, not a vacation.' We repeat this daily with our kids, both in the weeks leading up to our treks and while in the thick of it. It has been a game-changer in terms of expectation management. For a gal that was once prone to viewing getaways as a time to rest, recharge, and drink a mai tai on the beach, I've found that traveling with kids is very much the opposite. There's little in the way of rest (but everything in the way of renewal)."

—ERIN LOECHNER is the author of *Chasing Slow* and founder of OtherGoose.com, a home-schooling community for the preschool years. Based in Kansas, she has traveled the world with her husband Ken and their two children. You can find Erin on Instagram: @erinloechner.

will get you started creating on-the-road lessons with your children. Consider planning lessons that don't require a lot of extra supplies, like a visit to local playgrounds to discuss the different structures and how they are similar to or different from the playgrounds where you live.

CLASSROOM IN A BAG

A classroom in a bag makes it easy to incorporate learning moments into your travels. I recommend using a small cotton tote bag that can easily lay flat in a suitcase or be stowed away in a backpack to retrieve quickly when needed.

What to Pack:

- Small notebooks for lesson plans, drawing, and journaling

- Pencil case with pencils and erasers

- Maps of the location you're traveling to

- Small calendar with itinerary items and activities written out for your children

If you're traveling in a country where a foreign language is spoken, pack a small deck of flash cards with foreign words that children can learn and use easily.

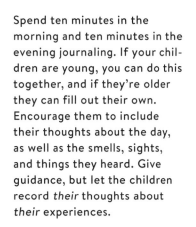

TRY THIS:

A Ten-Minute Travel Lesson

Spend ten minutes in the morning and ten minutes in the evening journaling. If your children are young, you can do this together, and if they're older they can fill out their own. Encourage them to include their thoughts about the day, as well as the smells, sights, and things they heard. Give guidance, but let the children record *their* thoughts about *their* experiences.

A Tool for Family Togetherness

FIND YOUR FIELD TRIP

Wherever your travels take you, around the world or to your backyard, I hope you see this book as a tool to carry with you on family outings. Share a copy with a friend with children, gift to the new parents in your life, or save it for your grandchildren. The nice thing about field trips is that they can be open-ended lessons. You can revisit them with your child many times, expanding and learning together a little more each time. That's what I hope this book does for you; I hope it's a starting point to help you on your lifelong adventure with your children.

RECIPES + FOODS TO TRY

ACTIVITIES + GAMES TO TRY

WORDS OR PHRASES WE'VE LEARNED
IN FOREIGN LANGUAGES

PLACES WE WANT TO VISIT AS A FAMILY

PLACES WE'VE BEEN AS A FAMILY

FAVORITE FAMILY FIELD TRIP MEMORIES

NOTES

DATE: _____ LOCATION: _____

NOTES

DATE: _____ LOCATION: _____

NOTES

DATE: _____   LOCATION: _____

NOTES

DATE: _____ LOCATION: _____

NOTES

NOTES

DATE: _____ LOCATION: _____

SKETCHES

SKETCHES

DATE: _____ LOCATION: _____

SKETCHES

DATE: _____ LOCATION: _____

SKETCHES

DATE: _____ LOCATION: _____

SKETCHES

DATE: _____ LOCATION: _____

SKETCHES

DATE: _____ LOCATION: _____

SKETCHES

DATE: _____ LOCATION: _____

SKETCHES

DATE: _____ LOCATION: _____

Resources:

There are so many amazing resources for teaching children about travel and culture. Here are some of my go-tos.

Books:

36 Hours by The New York Times

A Beetle Is Shy by Dianna Hutts Aston

A River by Marc Martin

Atlas of Adventures by Rachel Williams

Everything & Everywhere by Marc Martin

Hello NY by Julia Rothman

Here We Are by Oliver Jeffers

How to Raise a Wild Child by Scott D. Sampson

Last Stop on Market Street by Matt de la Peña

Let's Go Outside by Katja Spitzer

Lots by Marc Martin

Magnolia's Magnificent Map by Lauren Bradshaw

Maps by Aleksandra Mizielinska

Migrant by Maxine Trottier

Mindful Me by Whitney Stewart

My Big Barefoot Book of French & English Words by Sophie Fatus

Pancakes, Tacos, and Pizza series by Lotta Nieminen

People by Peter Spier

Play the Forest School Way by Peter Houghton and Jane Worroll

Sam and Dave Dig a Hole by Mac Barnett

See San Francisco by Victoria Smith

Smart About Sharks by Owen Davey

The 50 States by Sol Linero

The Golden Glow by Benjamin Flouw

The Map of Good Memories by Fran Nuño

This Is How We Do It by Matt Lamothe

This Is Mexico City by Abby Clason Low

This Way Watson by Claudia Pearson

Maps:

OMY maps

Small Adventures Journal

ZigZag City Guides

The New Voyager illustrated city guides for kids

Wildsam Field Guides

Herb Lester maps

City Maps Scratch-Off

CITI x Family

The Bitter Southerner Maps

Petite Passport Guides

Toys and Art Supplies:

pinch • toys

Huzi

Gathre playmats

Coloring Without Borders

Little-Biscuits Dress-Me Notepads

Lola & Lark Playpa rolls and rubber roads

Magna-Tiles

Tegu travel blocks

Colorforms

Mirus Toys via Etsy

Playforever cars

Blabla

Maileg

PlanToys

Mr. Boddington's Studio stationery sets

Olli Ella

Crack-open geodes

Websites for Traveling and Teaching:

swimminghole.com

teacherspayteachers.com

kidworldcitizen.org

khanacademy.org

somewhereslower.com

outschool.com

colearn.club

pinterest.com

freetoursbyfoot.com

kidandcoe.com

codecademy.com

readingeggs.com

studyladder.com

artforkidshub.com

seterra.com

Apps for Traveling and Teaching:

Airbnb

Audible

Bound Round

Citymaps2go

Compass

DailyArt

Elk travel currency converter

Exhibitionary

Explorer

Gas Buddy

Getaways

Get Outdoors by Coleman

Google Arts & Culture

Google Maps	Mobile Passport	Stamp
Google Trips	Mondly	Sygic Travel
Guides by Lonely Planet	NYC Subway	Tiqets
Hopper	Jetsetter	Trail Wallet
HotelTonight	PackPoint	TriPit
iNaturalist	Pocket Earth	Uber
iTunes U	Roadtrippers	Uber Eats
Kayak	SeeQr	Waypoint EDU
LouvreHD	SitOrSquat	Waze
MAPS.ME	Skyscanner	WhatsApp
Mezi	SoundCloud	Wunderlist

Thank-Yous

A HUGE THANKS TO:

All the wonderful people at Chronicle Books. Thank you to Rachel Hiles for being the most capable and thoughtful editor. You are truly so supportive and kind. I hope we can keep making books together. To Rachel Harrell and George Wylesol for your incredible design and illustrations. You both helped to make my dream book to write become my dream book to visually look at as well. And thank you to all the parents that offered up tips and advice through the Field Tips in this book. Your words are invaluable.

Thank you to my agent, Kim Perel, for believing in me endlessly. You are my agent and my friend and I'm glad I can call you both.

To Kori and Jason Hammel and Steve and Becky Drozd for teaching me how to travel with children. My years spent with both of your families only made me appreciate the idea of travel with my own child so much more. I love your families as my own.

To Lindsey Weidhorn and Kristen Ley. Together, with Kim Perel, you have believed in me, and I can't thank you enough for that.

To my friends around the country that have encouraged me, supported my ideas, and been the best of friends for so many years, I love you all. Jen Sperling, Christian Owens, Rachel Atkins, Kate and Cody Roebuck, Laura and Jed Roebuck, Jason Mann, Anna and Ben Avant, Brit McDanial, Kerri Sneed, Brandy Duffett, Sarah Gill, Mike, Lauren and Mallory Prater, Hannah and Heath Carpenter, Lauren Bradshaw, Diana Parks, Angela Parks Talarczky, Lauren Ziemski, Hannah Cooper, Erin Williams, Anne Sage, Kirk and Eva Jorgensen, Alison Powell, Ryan Kelly, Michelle Matthews, Sam Barbera, Anna Benefield, Courtney Webb, Meg Sutton, Chaney and Leah Nichols, Kate Woodrow, Joanna Hawley, and Kelly Jones.

To my Design*Sponge family, Grace Bonney and Julia Turshen, Kelli Kehler, Sofia Tuovinen, Lauren Day, Caitlin Kelch, and Garrett Fleming. I'm so thankful for your support and friendship.

To Y.Y.H. What would I do without our community? May I never find out, because nothing would feel as complete. I love you ladies and our times together.

To Camp Gwynn Valley in Brevard, NC. Thank you for encouraging wonder, adventure, and curiosity about the world throughout my childhood. I carry your lessons with me today.

To all of my Water Valley and Oxford friends. You are truly a magical community and I'm so happy to be surrounded by all of you daily. There are too many of you to mention by name, but you know who you are and I'm so thankful for your friendships.

To all of my family, both related and by marriage. I feel so fortunate and thankful to have you all in my life. To my in-laws, we were made to be family. I love you all so much. I wish my grandparents were still alive to see this book. The stories they shared with me from their world travels continue to inspire me.

To the families that travel the world with their children. Thank you for taking the time and energy to raise your own citizens of the world.

To my mom, Dorothy Abbott. I couldn't begin to tell you how thankful I am to you for taking the time and energy to teach me about the world, sometimes without even leaving home.

And finally to my loves, Sean and Tom Otis Kirkpatrick. There are no two other people that I'd want to travel the world with. From home and beyond. May our lives together always be a field trip.